Taste of Home's
MEALS IN MINUTES

Make Quick-and-Easy Meals That Will Satisfy Your Family

GATHERING YOUR FAMILY around the dinner table for a hearty, home-cooked meal doesn't have to be a thing of the past...even with today's busier-than-ever lifestyles.

Work, after-school activities, meetings and more may hinder your creativity in the kitchen, but with *Taste of Home's Meals in Minutes*, time is on your side.

You see, this convenient collection contains 53 complete meals—160 recipes in all—that can each be prepared in 30 minutes or less! Every recipe calls for ingredients you likely already have on hand, so go ahead and make a hearty, homemade meal for your family tonight.

You'll be amazed at how fast you can whip up any of these complete, home-style meals...which include a mouth-watering main dish, complementary side dish and down-home dessert.

When hectic days keep you hopping, serve slightly sweet Apricot Ham Steak, golden Potato Pancakes and Easy Rice Pudding. It's a speedy springtime meal impressive enough for Easter dinner (see page 28).

A patriotic spread featuring piled-high Turkey Hero sandwiches, Summertime Pasta Salad and Red, White and Blue Dessert can be made pronto and is sure to set off fireworks. (Recipes for this July Fourth feast begin on page 78.)

Instead of preparing an elaborate turkey dinner during the hectic holidays, turn to Herb-Glazed Turkey Slices, Rice Pilaf and creamy Pumpkin Mousse. You and your family are sure to give thanks for this fuss-free meal (featured on page 8).

Does dreaming up a winning winter dinner leave you out in the cold? Chase away chills in a hurry with sizzling Skillet Beef Stew, Parmesan Garlic Bread and Quick Fruit Crisp. (You'll find this cold-weather cuisine on page 22.)

That's just a small sample of the 53 complete meals compiled on the following pages. You can also mix and match the rapid recipes to come up with countless more quick-to-fix menus—enough for every day of the year and then some.

With *Taste of Home's Meals in Minutes*, it's easy to sit down to a well-rounded meal with your family...even on your busiest days!

Pictured on Front Cover: Top to bottom, Fruit-Topped Almond Cream, Meat Loaf Hamburgers and Microwave German Potato Salad (all recipes on page 49).

Pictured on Back Cover: Top to bottom, Flaky Garlic Rolls, Peppermint Mousse and Easy Italian Chicken (all recipes on page 13).

Taste of Home's
MEALS IN MINUTES
A sample of what's inside...

**A Quick Way to
Start the Day (p. 16)**

**Stir-Fry makes
Supper Simple (p. 35)**

**Family-Pleasing Feast
In a Flash (p. 72)**

**Fall Fare to Harvest
Compliments (p. 80)**

Editors: Jean Steiner, Heidi Reuter Lloyd
Art Director: Ellen Lloyd
Food Editor: Janaan Cunningham
Associate Food Editors: Coleen Martin, Diane Werner
Senior Recipe Editor: Sue A. Jurack
Associate Editors: Susan Uphill, Julie Schnittka
Food Photography Artist: Stephanie Marchese
Photo Studio Manager: Anne Schimmel

© 2002 Reiman Media Group, Inc.
5400 S. 60th St., Greendale WI 53129
International Standard Book Number: 0-89821-357-6
Library of Congress Control Number: 2002095943

Delicious Dinner Warms Heart and Soul

WHEN OTHER DUTIES keep your time in the kitchen to a minimum, a satisfying fast-to-fix meal is the perfect treat to give yourself and your family!

The complete-meal menu here is made up of favorite recipes shared by three great cooks. You can have everything ready to serve in about 30 minutes.

Salisbury Steak is shared by Carol Callahan of Rome, Georgia. "This meat dish can be made in 25 minutes," she assures, "or made ahead and reheated with the gravy in the microwave."

Continues Carol, "I often double the recipe and freeze one batch of cooked steaks and gravy for an even faster meal on an especially busy night."

Quick Carrots is a versatile colorful side dish from Florence Jacoby. This Granite Falls, Minnesota cook reports that the carrots and green onions are a flavorful combination your family is sure to enjoy.

Banana Pudding Dessert comes from Hazel Merrill of Greenville, South Carolina. "This creamy dessert with mild banana taste is 'comfort food' that tastes like you fussed," Hazel says.

servings. **Nutritional Analysis:** One serving (prepared with low-fat gravy and skim milk and without salt or noodles) equals 248 calories, 205 mg sodium, 66 mg cholesterol, 9 gm carbohydrate, 25 gm protein, 12 gm fat. **Diabetic Exchanges:** 3 meat, 1/2 starch, 1/2 vegetable.

Quick Carrots

　2 cups fresh *or* frozen sliced carrots
　1 tablespoon butter *or* margarine
　2 tablespoons sliced green onions
　1 tablespoon water
1/4 teaspoon salt
Chopped fresh parsley

In a saucepan, combine the first five ingredients. Cover and simmer for 8-10 minutes or until the carrots are crisp-tender. Sprinkle with parsley. **Yield:** 4 servings.

Salisbury Steak

✓ Uses less fat, sugar or salt. Includes Nutritional Analysis and Diabetic Exchanges.

　1 egg white, lightly beaten
1/3 cup chopped onion
1/4 cup crushed saltines
　2 tablespoons milk
　1 tablespoon prepared horseradish
1/4 teaspoon salt, optional
1/8 teaspoon pepper
　1 pound lean ground beef
　1 jar (12 ounces) beef gravy
1-1/4 to 1-1/2 cups sliced fresh mushrooms
　2 tablespoons water
Hot cooked noodles, optional

In a bowl, combine the egg white, onion, cracker crumbs, milk, horseradish, salt if desired and pepper. Add beef; mix well. Shape into four oval patties. Fry in a skillet over medium heat for 10-12 minutes or until cooked through, turning once. Remove patties and keep warm. Add gravy, mushrooms and water to skillet; heat for 3-5 minutes. Serve over patties and noodles if desired. **Yield:** 4

Banana Pudding Dessert

1-1/4 cups cold water
　1 can (14 ounces) sweetened condensed milk
　1 package (3.4 ounces) instant vanilla pudding mix
　2 cups whipped topping
　24 to 32 vanilla wafers
　3 large firm bananas, sliced

In a large bowl, combine water, milk and pudding mix; beat on low speed for 2 minutes. Chill for 5 minutes. Fold in the whipped topping. In individual dessert dishes, layer wafers, pudding, bananas and more pudding. Top each with a wafer. Chill until serving. **Yield:** 6-8 servings.

> ### Vivid Veggies
> For lovely looking vegetable dishes, add a bit of vinegar to the water when cooking. This trick helps all vegetables keep their fresh, bright color.

Cookout Classics

SUMMERTIME…and the cooking is easy! Just fire up the grill for a good old-fashioned barbecue featuring sizzling Garlic Grilled Steaks. With a tangy marinade and assortment of fresh produce, Zesty Vegetable Skewers are sure to disappear in a hurry. Cool and creamy Cheesecake Dip for sweet strawberries provides a perfectly happy ending to this flavorful fare. The recipes are from the *Taste of Home* Test Kitchen.

Garlic Grilled Steaks

For a mouth-watering change of taste at your next barbecue, take steak to new flavor heights by basting your choice of cuts with a great garlicky blend.

```
10 garlic cloves
1-1/2 teaspoons salt
    2 tablespoons olive or vegetable oil
    1 tablespoon lemon juice
    2 teaspoons Worcestershire sauce
1/2 teaspoon pepper
    4 New York strip or rib eye steaks
        (8 ounces and 1-1/4 inches thick)
```

In a small bowl, mash garlic with salt to form a paste. Add the oil, lemon juice, Worcestershire sauce and pepper; mix well. Grill the steaks over medium-hot heat, turning once and brushing with garlic mixture during the last few minutes of cooking. Allow approximately 11-12 minutes for rare, 13-14 minutes for medium and 15-16 minutes for well-done. **Yield:** 4 servings.

Zesty Vegetable Skewers

Grilling is a delightful way of preparing the season's freshest produce. The zesty Italian marinade adds just the right amount of spice to the appealing assortment of vegetables.

```
    1 garlic clove
    1 teaspoon salt
1/3 cup olive or vegetable oil
    3 tablespoons lemon juice
    1 teaspoon Italian seasoning
1/4 teaspoon pepper
    8 medium fresh mushrooms
    2 small zucchini, sliced 1/2 inch thick
    2 small onions, cut into sixths
    8 cherry tomatoes
```

In a small bowl, mash garlic with salt to form a paste. Stir in oil, lemon juice, Italian seasoning and pepper. Thread the mushrooms, zucchini, onions and tomatoes alternately onto skewers; place in a shallow baking pan. Pour garlic mixture over kabobs; let stand for 15 minutes. Grill for 10-15 minutes, turning frequently, or until vegetables are just tender. **Yield:** 4 servings.

Cheesecake Dip

When you're in the mood for something sweet, but you want to keep it light, this simple dip really hits the spot. Dipping fresh plump strawberries in the cool and creamy concoction is a fun and delicious way to eat dessert.

    4 ounces cream cheese, softened
1/3 cup sour cream
    3 tablespoons confectioners' sugar
    1 tablespoon milk
1/4 teaspoon almond extract
    1 pint fresh strawberries
1/4 cup graham cracker crumbs

In a mixing bowl, beat cream cheese until smooth. Add the sour cream, sugar, milk and extract; mix until smooth. Transfer to a serving bowl. Place the strawberries and crumbs in separate serving bowls. Dip strawberries into cheesecake mixture, then into crumbs. **Yield:** about 1 cup.

Avoid a Sticky Situation
To keep your meat from sticking on the grill, brush the grill's grid surface with vegetable oil.

Make It 'Turkey Day'...Any Day

YOU'LL be showered with "Thanks!" when you serve this succulent supper from the *Taste of Home* Test Kitchen. Herb-Glazed Turkey Slices let you enjoy wonderful fowl without preparing the whole turkey. For lighter side dishes that are full of flavor, try Rice Pilaf and your favorite vegetables, like carrots and brussels sprouts. Pumpkin Mousse is as easy as pie to prepare.

Herb-Glazed Turkey Slices

In the mood for a taste of turkey, but don't have time to prepare a whole bird? Here's the perfect solution! These savory slices—and easy-to-prepare herb glaze—offer the goodness of turkey in a hurry.

    1 package (about 1-1/4 pounds) turkey
      breast slices (1/4 inch thick)
    1 tablespoon vegetable oil
 1/2 cup chicken broth
 1/2 cup apple juice
    1 tablespoon honey
    1 tablespoon Dijon mustard
 1/2 teaspoon salt
 1/4 teaspoon *each* dried basil, rosemary and
      garlic powder
    1 tablespoon cornstarch
    1 tablespoon water
**Hot cooked brussels sprouts and carrots,
optional**

In a large skillet, brown turkey slices in oil. Combine broth, apple juice, honey, mustard, salt, basil, rosemary and garlic powder; pour over turkey. Cover and simmer for 8 minutes or until the turkey is no longer pink. Mix the cornstarch and water; stir into skillet. Cook and stir until thickened and bubbly. Serve with brussels sprouts and carrots if desired. **Yield:** 4 servings.

Look, Ma! No Hands!

The next time you're struggling to fill a storage bag, try this easy method. Line a tall drinking glass with the bag, and fold the top of the bag over the rim of the glass. With the glass holding the bag, your hands are free to fill it.

Rice Pilaf

Onion soup mix and frozen peas really "rev up" your rice in this recipe. This side dish is a nice alternative to potatoes and complements turkey or any main course.

    1 cup uncooked long grain rice
    1 tablespoon vegetable oil
1-1/2 to 2 tablespoons dry onion soup mix
 1/4 teaspoon pepper
1-2/3 cups boiling water
    1 cup frozen peas

In a large skillet, brown rice in oil, stirring constantly. Blend in soup mix and pepper. Stir in water; bring to a boil. Reduce heat; cover and simmer for 15 minutes or until the rice is tender. Stir

in peas. Cover and cook for 5 minutes. Serve immediately. **Yield:** 4 servings.

Pumpkin Mousse

If you've had your fill of pumpkin pie, this cool and creamy mousse is just right for you. Its light and fluffy texture won't make you feel "stuffed" after your favorite turkey dinner.

   1 package (8 ounces) cream cheese, softened
1/4 cup sugar

   1 can (15 ounces) solid-pack pumpkin
   1 package (3.4 ounces) instant vanilla pudding mix
   2 teaspoons pumpkin pie spice
   1 cup cold milk
1-3/4 cups whipped topping
   24 gingersnaps

In a mixing bowl, beat cream cheese and sugar until smooth. Beat in pumpkin. Add pudding mix and pie spice; mix well. Gradually beat in milk. Fold in whipped topping. Spoon about 1/4 cup each into serving dishes. Crumble 2 gingersnaps over each. Divide remaining pumpkin mixture among dishes. Garnish with a whole gingersnap. Chill until serving. Refrigerate leftovers. **Yield:** 8 servings.

Spicy Supper Kindles Family Memories

IS YOUR FAMILY in the mood for an authentic Mexican-style meal and you have only a few minutes until mealtime?

You don't need to resort to fast food when the clock is ticking closer to dinnertime. With these family favorites, a wholesome, hearty meal is within reach!

Quick Chili comes from Jean Ward of Montgomery, Texas, who's made this mild-tasting and hearty main dish for more than 30 years to the delight of her family and friends.

Canned soup and beans are the secrets to the recipe's rapid preparation. For even faster meal making, brown, drain and freeze the ground beef when time allows. When ready to use, just combine frozen cooked beef with the other ingredients and simmer as directed.

South-of-the-Border Sandwiches, shared by Karen Byrd of Las Vegas, Nevada, are fun and filling with a tasty combination of ingredients. "My mom and her dear friend, Betty, came up with this recipe many years ago, and I'm still using it," Karen relates. "Of course with seven kids in the family, Mom would have to double and sometimes triple the recipe!"

Adds Karen, "My mom grew up in Wisconsin. But after she and Dad moved here in the 1950s, she quickly learned from her mother-in-law how to prepare many Mexican dishes. In fact, I recall eating beans and tortillas almost every night with dinner."

Peanut Butter Sundaes are a peanutty change of pace from the traditional ice cream sundae with chocolate sauce, assures Susan Mowery of Newville, Pennsylvania. This delicious recipe proves that even a quick meal doesn't have to go without dessert.

A little bit of this sauce goes a long way to please every sweet tooth in your family. For a little variation, sprinkle some chocolate chips on top.

Quick Chili

 Uses less fat, sugar or salt. Includes Nutritional Analysis and Diabetic Exchanges.

1 pound ground beef
1 can (10-3/4 ounces) condensed tomato soup, undiluted
1 can (15 ounces) chili beans in gravy, undrained
2 to 3 teaspoons chili powder
1/2 cup water, optional

In a saucepan, brown the ground beef; drain. Add soup, beans and chili powder. Reduce heat. Cover and simmer for 20 minutes. Add water if a thinner soup is desired. **Yield:** 4 servings. **Nutritional Analysis:** One serving (prepared with lean ground beef and low-fat tomato soup) equals 344 calories, 341 mg sodium, 108 mg cholesterol, 24 gm carbohydrate, 31 gm protein, 5 gm fat. **Diabetic Exchanges:** 3 meat, 1-1/2 starch.

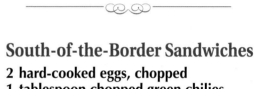

South-of-the-Border Sandwiches

2 hard-cooked eggs, chopped
1 tablespoon chopped green chilies
1/3 cup salsa
1 green onion, sliced
2 tablespoons sliced ripe olives
Dash *each* salt, pepper and ground cumin
1 cup (4 ounces) shredded cheddar cheese
4 French *or* submarine rolls, split

In a large bowl, mix eggs, chilies, salsa, onion, olives and seasonings. Fold in cheese. Spoon 1/2 cup onto bottom of rolls. Replace tops; wrap each sandwich tightly in foil. Bake at 350° for 20 minutes. **Yield:** 4 servings.

Peanut Butter Sundaes

1 cup sugar
1/2 cup water
1/2 cup creamy peanut butter
Vanilla ice cream
Salted peanuts, optional

In a saucepan, combine sugar and water. Bring to a boil; boil 1 minute or until sugar is dissolved. Remove from the heat; stir in peanut butter. Place in a blender; cover and blend on high until smooth. Cool slightly; pour over ice cream. Sprinkle with peanuts if desired. Refrigerate any leftovers. **Yield:** 1-1/2 cups sauce.

Bring a Taste of Italy To Your Table

NOTHING WARMS your spirit on a cold evening like a hot and hearty meal. Plus, it's a welcome sight for you and your family after a busy day at work, school or play.

This easy-to-make Italian dinner is made up of favorite recipes shared by three busy cooks and combined in our test kitchen.

Easy Italian Chicken, from Joan Rose of Langley, British Columbia, is a lovely fresh-tasting main course you can serve with pride and without fuss.

"When we want a hearty Italian dish but I don't want to spend hours cooking, this is the recipe I choose," Joan conveys. "Boneless skinless chicken breasts are convenient to have in the freezer because they thaw and cook quickly. Plus, I always have the other ingredients in my pantry."

Flaky Garlic Rolls are a fun and tasty way to dress up handy refrigerator biscuits. "Hot from the oven, these rolls are great alongside any meat and are also super with soup or as an evening snack," assures Peggy Burdick from Burlington, Michigan.

"Garlic bread tastes especially nice with this saucy chicken and spaghetti."

Peppermint Mousse is a refreshing, mildly minty dessert suggested by Julie Moyer, from Union Grove, Wisconsin. "Although I've been known to prepare this delicious dessert throughout the year, it's a wonderful way to end a holiday meal," Julie remarks.

Easy Italian Chicken

✓ Uses less fat, sugar or salt. Includes Nutritional Analysis and Diabetic Exchanges.

- **4 boneless skinless chicken breast halves**
- **1 can (14-1/2 ounces) Italian stewed tomatoes**
- **1 can (4 ounces) mushroom stems and pieces, drained**
- **1/2 teaspoon dried basil**
- **1/4 teaspoon garlic powder**
- **1 tablespoon cornstarch**
- **1/3 cup cold water**
- **Hot cooked spaghetti**

In a large skillet coated with nonstick cooking spray, cook chicken for 5-6 minutes on each side or until the juices run clear. Meanwhile, in a saucepan over medium heat, bring tomatoes, mushrooms, basil and garlic powder to a boil. Combine cornstarch and water; add to tomato mixture. Return to a boil; cook and stir for 2 minutes. Serve chicken over spaghetti; top with the tomato sauce. **Yield:** 4 servings. **Nutritional Analysis:** One serving (prepared with no-salt-added stewed tomatoes and calculated without spaghetti) equals 177 calories, 178 mg sodium, 73 mg cholesterol, 7 gm carbohydrate, 28 gm protein, 3 gm fat. **Diabetic Exchanges:** 3 very lean meat, 2 vegetable.

Flaky Garlic Rolls

- **1 tube (6 ounces) refrigerated flaky biscuits**
- **1 to 2 tablespoons butter *or* margarine, melted**
- **1/4 to 1/2 teaspoon garlic salt**

Separate each biscuit into three pieces; place on a greased baking sheet. Brush with butter; sprinkle with garlic salt. Bake at 400° for 8-10 minutes or until golden brown. Serve warm. **Yield:** 15 rolls.

Peppermint Mousse

- **1 envelope unflavored gelatin**
- **2 tablespoons cold water**
- **1 cup milk**
- **4 ounces chocolate-covered peppermint patties**
- **1/2 teaspoon vanilla extract**
- **1/4 teaspoon salt**
- **1 cup whipping cream, whipped**
- **Fresh mint and additional peppermint patties, optional**

In a saucepan, sprinkle gelatin over water; let stand for 1 minute. Add milk and peppermint patties; stir over low heat for 5 minutes or until candies and gelatin are dissolved. Add vanilla and salt. Pour into a mixing bowl; place in freezer for 15-20 minutes, stirring frequently until the mixture is cooled and thickened. Beat for 1 minute or until fluffy. Fold in whipped cream. Spoon into serving dishes. Garnish with mint and peppermint patties if desired. **Yield:** 4-6 servings.

Busy Cooks Depend on Classic Combination

WHEN TIME'S short and hunger's high, you can always rely on soup and a sandwich. Whether you serve it as a hearty lunch or light supper, the comforting, tasty flavor just can't be beat.

Add a pretty dessert that can be made pronto, and you have a complete family-pleasing meal in no time at all.

Flavorful and filling, Sausage Bean Soup from Marlene Muckenhirn of Delano, Minnesota calls for canned beans and quick-cooking Italian sausage, so it needs to simmer for only a few minutes instead of a few hours.

Italian Grilled Cheese sandwiches are a delicious, dressed-up version of the traditional favorite. "The pocket of melted mozzarella or provolone cheese and a crisp crumb coating give these hot sandwiches a tasty twist," says Vera Ambroselli of Lehigh Acres, Florida. For added taste, use a combination of cheeses.

Pretty Cherry Parfaits are just the treat when you want to serve a dessert that's fast, lovely and scrumptious, assures Bernice Morris of Marshfield, Missouri.

Sausage Bean Soup

3/4 pound bulk Italian sausage
1/2 cup chopped onion
  1 garlic clove, minced
  1 can (15-1/2 ounces) butter beans, rinsed and drained
  1 can (15 ounces) black beans, rinsed and drained
  1 can (14-1/2 ounces) beef broth

Working with Dry Beans

When you do have time and you'd like to prepare Sausage Bean Soup using dry beans, keep in mind this simple substitution: 1 cup packaged dry beans (uncooked) equals about two 15-1/2-ounce cans of beans (drained).

Before using the dry beans, sort and rinse them. Place in a soup kettle; add enough water to cover by 2 inches. Bring to a boil; boil for 2 minutes. Remove from the heat; cover and let stand for 1 hour. Drain and rinse; discard liquid.

---

  1 can (14-1/2 ounces) diced tomatoes, undrained
  1 tablespoon minced fresh basil *or* 1 teaspoon dried basil
  2 tablespoons shredded Parmesan cheese

In a large saucepan, cook sausage, onion and garlic until the sausage is browned; drain. Add beans, broth, tomatoes and basil. Cover and simmer for 10 minutes. Sprinkle each serving with Parmesan cheese. **Yield:** 4-6 servings.

Italian Grilled Cheese

  4 slices Italian bread (1 inch thick)
  4 slices mozzarella *or* provolone cheese
  3 eggs
1/2 cup milk
3/4 teaspoon Italian seasoning
1/2 teaspoon garlic salt
2/3 cup Italian-seasoned bread crumbs

Cut a 3-in. pocket in each slice of bread; place a slice of cheese in each pocket. In a bowl, beat eggs, milk, Italian seasoning and garlic salt; soak bread for 2 minutes on each side. Coat with the bread crumbs. Cook on a greased hot griddle until golden brown on both sides. **Yield:** 4 servings.

Pretty Cherry Parfaits

  1 can (21 ounces) cherry pie filling
1/4 teaspoon almond extract
  1 cup (8 ounces) sour cream
  1 cup cold milk
  1 package (3.4 ounces) instant vanilla pudding mix
Whipped topping, chopped almonds and fresh mint, optional

Combine pie filling and extract; set aside. In a mixing bowl, combine sour cream and milk. Stir in pudding mix; beat on low speed for 2 minutes. Spoon half into parfait glasses; top with half of the pie filling. Repeat layers. Garnish with whipped topping, almonds and mint if desired. Refrigerate until serving. **Yield:** 4-6 servings.

A Quick and Tasty Way To Start the Day

COOKING UP a big hearty breakfast for your brood is a great way to help them start their day off right. But there are some days when time is short or you and your family just want to be able to make the most of a beautiful morning.

On those days, turn to this brisk, delicious breakfast that will help your family get going in no time. You can have everything ready to serve in about half an hour!

Breakfast Burritos are a fun and filling way to serve scrambled eggs, and the zippy flavor will wake up your taste buds, assures Brenda Spann of Granger, Indiana, who shares her recipe.

Potatoes O'Brien comes from Nila Towler of Baird, Texas. "I usually serve these colorful potatoes for breakfast," notes Nila. "But they're great as a tasty potato side dish for just about any meal. My family often asks me to prepare them instead of regular fried potatoes."

Lemon Blueberry Biscuits are easy to make and a treat to eat. Kristin Dallum of Vancouver, Washington says she got the recipe from her mother, who's a wonderful baker.

Breakfast Burritos

    1 pound bulk pork sausage
    1 small onion, chopped
1/2 green pepper, chopped
    1 can (4 ounces) mushroom stems and
        pieces, drained
    8 flour tortillas (7 inches), warmed
    6 eggs, beaten
    1 cup (4 ounces) shredded cheddar cheese
Salsa, optional

In a skillet, brown sausage. Drain, discarding all but 2 tablespoons drippings. Add onion, green pepper and mushrooms; saute until tender. Meanwhile, in another skillet or in the microwave, scramble the eggs. Place an equal amount of sausage mixture on each tortilla; cover with an equal amount of eggs and 2 tablespoons of cheese. Fold bottom of tortilla over filling and roll up. Serve with salsa if desired. **Yield:** 4 servings.

Potatoes O'Brien

1/2 cup chopped onion
1/2 cup chopped green pepper
1/2 cup chopped sweet red pepper
    4 medium red potatoes, cubed
    3 tablespoons vegetable oil
1/4 cup beef broth
1/2 teaspoon Worcestershire sauce
    1 teaspoon salt

In a skillet over medium heat, saute the onion, peppers and potatoes in oil for 4 minutes. Combine broth, Worcestershire sauce and salt; pour over vegetables. Cover and cook for 10 minutes or until potatoes are tender, stirring occasionally. Uncover and cook until liquid is absorbed, about 3 minutes. **Yield:** 4 servings.

Lemon Blueberry Biscuits

    2 cups all-purpose flour
1/3 cup sugar
    2 teaspoons baking powder
1/2 teaspoon baking soda
1/4 teaspoon salt
    1 carton (8 ounces) lemon yogurt
    1 egg, lightly beaten
1/4 cup butter *or* margarine, melted
    1 teaspoon grated lemon peel
    1 cup fresh *or* frozen blueberries
GLAZE:
1/2 cup confectioners' sugar
    1 tablespoon lemon juice
1/2 teaspoon grated lemon peel

In a large bowl, combine dry ingredients. Combine yogurt, egg, butter and lemon peel; stir into dry ingredients just until moistened. Fold in blueberries. Drop by tablespoonfuls onto a greased baking sheet. Bake at 400° for 15-18 minutes or until lightly browned. Combine glaze ingredients; drizzle over warm biscuits. **Yield:** 1 dozen.

Round Up the Family For Ham Rolls!

AFTER SPENDING hours in the kitchen baking holiday breads, muffins and fruitcakes, you deserve time to relax!

So when your family starts calling for dinner, reach for the hearty ham featured here. The fabulous flavor will be just the nourishment you need before the next marathon session of baking!

Apricot Ham Rolls, from Carolyn Hannay of Antioch, Tennessee, are both speedy and special. "This is the kind of hearty dish we 10 kids would devour after doing chores on our parents' farm," Carolyn recalls. "Mom always had lots of hungry mouths to appreciate her good food. When I'm short on cooking time, I rely on this tasty recipe."

Broccoli Stir-Fry is a great way to dress up a nutritious vegetable. Reports Susan Davis of Vernon Hills, Illinois, "As a wife and mother who also works full-time, I'm pleased to pass along this easy recipe to other busy cooks. Broccoli stir-fried with lemon pepper makes a mouth-watering side dish."

Microwave Cherry Crisp uses a time-saving method to produce a treat with old-fashioned flavor, says Debra Morello of Edwards, California. She assures, "It tastes just like the old-time 'crisp' with half the fuss and mess. For a little variety, you can substitute other fruit pie fillings—including apple, blueberry and peach—for the cherry pie filling."

Apricot Ham Rolls

1-2/3 cups apricot nectar, *divided*
    1 tablespoon Dijon mustard
  1/2 teaspoon salt
    1 cup uncooked instant rice
    2 tablespoons minced fresh parsley
    8 thin slices fully cooked ham
    2 tablespoons maple syrup

In a saucepan over medium heat, combine 1-1/3 cups apricot nectar, mustard and salt; bring to a boil. Stir in rice. Remove from the heat; cover and let stand for 6-8 minutes or until the liquid is absorbed. Add parsley and fluff with fork. Place about 1/4 cup of rice mixture on each slice of ham. Overlap two opposite corners of ham over rice mixture; secure with a toothpick. In a large skillet over medium-high heat, combine syrup and remaining nectar; bring to a boil. Add ham rolls; reduce heat. Cover and simmer for about 5 minutes or until heated through, basting occasionally with the sauce. Remove the toothpicks before serving. **Yield:** 4 servings.

Broccoli Stir-Fry

    3 cups fresh broccoli florets
  1/4 cup butter *or* margarine
1-1/2 teaspoons lemon-pepper seasoning

In a skillet over medium-high heat, stir-fry broccoli in butter and lemon pepper until crisp-tender, about 2-3 minutes. **Yield:** 4 servings.

Microwave Cherry Crisp

    1 can (21 ounces) cherry pie filling
  3/4 cup packed brown sugar
  2/3 cup quick-cooking oats
  1/3 cup all-purpose flour
  1/4 cup cold butter *or* margarine
Vanilla ice cream, optional

Spoon pie filling into a greased 9-in. microwave-safe pie plate. In a bowl, combine brown sugar, oats and flour; cut in butter until crumbly. Sprinkle over filling. Microwave on high for 12-14 minutes. Serve warm with ice cream if desired. **Yield:** 4-6 servings. **Editor's Note:** This recipe was tested in a 700-watt microwave.

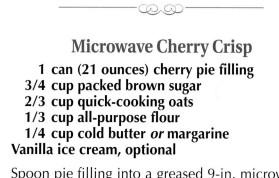

Selecting and Storing Broccoli

When purchasing fresh broccoli, look for firm stalks with a deep green color and heads that are tightly packed. Stalks with wilted leaves and florets that are light green or yellow are past their prime. Fresh broccoli can be stored in a plastic bag in the refrigerator for up to 4 days. To store broccoli longer, blanche it and freeze for up to 1 year.

Folks Will Have Fun
Dipping into Chicken Di[r]

WHEN CABIN FEVER strikes at your house, invite friends over for a spur-of-the moment gathering. You can plan the party in short order with "fast foods".

The crowd-pleasing fare here can be ready to serve in just 30 minutes.

Oven Chicken Fingers are tender, golden strips of breaded chicken with two tempting sauces for dipping. The recipe comes from Mary Peterson of Charlestown, Rhode Island.

Broccoli Noodle Side Dish is colorful and satisfying, relates Louise Saluti of Sandwich, Massachusetts.

Raspberry Mallow Pie is a delightful way to end a quick-to-fix meal. The recipe is shared by Judie Anglen of Riverton, Wyoming.

Oven Chicken Fingers

- 1 cup Italian bread crumbs
- 2 tablespoons grated Parmesan cheese
- 1 garlic clove, minced
- 1/4 cup vegetable oil
- 6 boneless skinless chicken breast halves

CRANBERRY ORANGE SAUCE:
- 1/4 cup sugar
- 2 teaspoons cornstarch
- 1/2 cup fresh or frozen cranberries
- 1/2 cup orange juice
- 1/4 cup water

HONEY MUSTARD SAUCE:
- 2 tablespoons cornstarch
- 1 cup water, divided
- 1/2 cup honey
- 1/4 cup prepared mustard

In a large resealable plastic bag, combine bread crumbs and Parmesan cheese; set aside. In a small bowl, combine garlic and oil. Flatten the chicken to 1/2-in. thickness; cut into 1-in.-wide strips. Dip strips in oil; place in bag with crumb mixture and toss to coat. Place on a greased baking sheet. Bake at 350° for 20 minutes or until golden brown. Meanwhile, combine the sugar and cornstarch in a saucepan. Add cranberries, orange juice and water; bring to a boil over medium heat, stirring constantly. Cook 2-3 minutes more, stirring to crush the berries. For honey mustard sauce, dissolve cornstarch in 1 tablespoon water in a saucepan. Add honey, mustard and remaining water; bring to a boil over medium heat. Boil for 1 minute, stirring constantly. Serve sauces with chicken for dipping. **Yield:** 6 servings.

Broccoli Noodle Side Dish

☑ Uses less fat, sugar or salt. Includes Nutritional Analysis and Diabetic Exchanges.

- 6 cups (8 ounces) uncooked wide noodles
- 3 to 4 garlic cloves, minced
- 1/4 cup olive or vegetable oil
- 4 cups broccoli florets (about 1 pound)
- 1/2 pound fresh mushrooms, thinly sliced
- 1/2 teaspoon dried thyme
- 1/4 teaspoon pepper
- 1 teaspoon salt, optional

Cook the noodles according to package directions. Meanwhile, in a skillet, saute garlic in oil until tender. Add broccoli; saute for 4 minutes or until crisp-tender. Add mushrooms, thyme, pepper and salt if desired; saute for 2-3 minutes. Drain noodles and add to broccoli mixture. Stir gently over low heat until heated through. **Yield:** 8 servings. **Nutritional Analysis:** One 1-cup serving (prepared without salt) equals 167 calories, 12 mg sodium, 23 mg cholesterol, 20 gm carbohydrate, 5 gm protein, 8 gm fat. **Diabetic Exchanges:** 1-1/2 fat, 1 starch, 1 vegetable.

Raspberry Mallow Pie

- 35 large marshmallows
- 1/2 cup milk
- 1 package (10 ounces) sweetened frozen raspberries, undrained
- 1 carton (8 ounces) frozen whipped topping, thawed
- 1 graham cracker crust (9 inches)

In a large microwave-safe bowl, combine marshmallows and milk. Cook on high for 1-2 minutes; stir until smooth. Stir in raspberries. Fold in the whipped topping. Pour into crust. Refrigerate or freeze. **Yield:** 6-8 servings. **Editor's Note:** This recipe was tested in a 700-watt microwave.

A Winning Winter Dinner

AFTER PLAYING in a winter wonderland, your family will build up big appetites. Made with hearty ingredients, sizzling Skillet Beef Stew—like the individual portion shown at right—and fresh-from-the-oven Parmesan Garlic Bread are guaranteed to chase away Jack Frost in a hurry! For a sweet finale to this satisfying meal from our Test Kitchen, why not serve Quick Fruit Crisp and mugs of hot cocoa?

Skillet Beef Stew

Think you can't prepare a hot and hearty stew in under 30 minutes? Well you can! This super stew recipe uses frozen vegetables and prepared gravy, plus it cooks on the stove, so you can serve up steaming bowlsful in no time.

- 1 pound sirloin steak
- 2 tablespoons vegetable oil
- 1 package (16 ounces) frozen vegetables for stew
- 1 jar (12 ounces) beef gravy
- 2 tablespoons Worcestershire sauce
- 1/2 teaspoon dried thyme
- 1/4 teaspoon pepper
- 1/4 teaspoon garlic powder

Cut steak into 2-in. x 1/4-in. strips. Heat oil in a large skillet; brown meat over medium-high heat for 5 minutes or until no longer pink. Drain if necessary. Stir in remaining ingredients; bring to a boil. Reduce heat; cover and simmer for 15 minutes or until heated through. **Yield:** 4 servings.

Parmesan Garlic Bread

Dress up ordinary French bread by topping it with butter, Parmesan cheese and seasonings. It's a quick side dish that will complement the beef stew or most any meal. But don't expect leftovers...your family will have a hard time stopping at just one slice!

- 1/4 cup butter *or* margarine, softened
- 1/4 cup olive *or* vegetable oil
- 1/4 cup grated Parmesan cheese
- 2 garlic cloves
- 4 sprigs fresh parsley
- 1/2 teaspoon lemon-pepper seasoning
- 1 small loaf (8 ounces) French bread

In a mixing bowl or food processor, blend butter, oil and Parmesan cheese. Add garlic, parsley and lemon pepper; mix or process until smooth. Slice the bread on the diagonal but not all the way through, leaving slices attached at the bottom. Spread butter mixture on one side of each slice and over the top. Wrap in foil and bake at 400° for 15-20 minutes. **Yield:** 4 servings.

Quick Fruit Crisp

Fruit crisps often take time to prepare, what with slicing the fruit and baking in the oven. But this quick and easy dessert uses canned pie filling and is cooked in a skillet! Serve it alone or with a scoop of ice cream.

1 can (21 ounces) peach, apple *or* cherry
  pie filling
1 tablespoon lemon juice
1 cup Fruit & Fibre cereal
1 tablespoon butter *or* margarine
1 tablespoon sugar
1/4 teaspoon ground cinnamon
Vanilla ice cream, optional

In a medium skillet, heat pie filling and lemon juice over medium heat for 5 minutes or until bubbly, stirring occasionally. Meanwhile, place cereal in a resealable plastic bag; crush slightly with a rolling pin. In a small skillet, melt butter. Stir in cereal, sugar and cinnamon; cook and stir for 2-3 minutes. Sprinkle over the fruit mixture. Serve warm with ice cream if desired. **Yield:** 4 servings.

Warm-Weather Meal With Mouth-Watering Appeal

WHETHER you're working in the garden or relaxing in the shade, summertime tempts even the most avid cooks to spend more time outdoors and less in the kitchen.

Since fresh air builds hearty appetites, what you will surely need is this speedy and nutritious meal that satisfies.

Garbanzo Cucumber Salad is shared by Sharon Semph of Victorville, California. "This crisp, refreshing salad is great for an outdoor barbecue or potluck," Sharon suggests.

Tasty Turkey Sub makes a delicious warm-weather main dish, says Steven Scott of Cameron, West Virginia, who sent the recipe.

Orange Sauce for Angel Food Cake comes from Karen Bourne of Magrath, Alberta. It's a tasty way to end a summer meal—without turning on the oven.

Garbanzo Cucumber Salad

☑ Uses less fat, sugar or salt. Includes Nutritional Analysis and Diabetic Exchanges.

    1 can (15 ounces) garbanzo beans, rinsed
      and drained
    1 medium cucumber, sliced and quartered
  1/2 cup sliced ripe olives
  1/3 cup chopped red onion
  1/4 cup minced fresh parsley
    3 tablespoons vegetable oil
    3 tablespoons cider or red wine vinegar
    1 tablespoon sugar
    1 tablespoon lemon juice
    2 garlic cloves, minced
  1/2 teaspoon grated lemon peel
  1/4 teaspoon salt, optional
  1/8 teaspoon pepper

In a medium bowl, combine beans, cucumber, olives, onion and parsley. In a jar with tight-fitting lid, combine remaining ingredients; shake well. Pour over vegetables and toss. Serve immediately or chill up to 24 hours. **Yield:** 8 servings.
Nutritional Analysis: One 1/2-cup serving (prepared without salt) equals 145 calories, 251 mg sodium, 0 cholesterol, 18 gm carbohydrate, 4 gm protein, 8 gm fat. **Diabetic Exchanges:** 1-1/2 fat, 1 starch.

Tasty Turkey Sub

    1 loaf (1 pound) French bread
  1/3 cup blue cheese salad dressing
  1/3 cup mayonnaise
    2 tablespoons Dijon mustard
    1 pound smoked or cooked turkey, thinly
      sliced
   12 bacon strips, cooked and drained
    1 avocado, thinly sliced
    6 tomato slices (1/4 inch thick)
Shredded lettuce

Halve bread lengthwise. Spread blue cheese dressing on cut side of top of bread. Combine mayonnaise and mustard; spread on cut side of bottom of bread. Layer with turkey, bacon, avocado, tomato and lettuce. Cover with top half of bread. Serve immediately. **Yield:** 6 servings.

Orange Sauce for Angel Food Cake

1-1/4 cups water
    1 can (6 ounces) frozen orange juice
      concentrate, thawed
    1 package (3.4 ounces) instant vanilla
      pudding mix
    1 cup whipped topping
    1 prepared angel food cake, sliced

In a mixing bowl, combine water, orange juice concentrate and pudding. Beat on low until mixed; beat on high for 2 minutes. Whisk in whipped topping. Spoon over cake slices. Store leftovers in the refrigerator. **Yield:** 2-3/4 cups sauce.

No-Fry Bacon

As an alternative to frying bacon, lay the strips on a jelly roll pan and bake at 350° for about 30 minutes. Prepared this way, bacon comes out crisp and flat. Plus, the pan cleans easily, and there's no stovetop splattering.

Oven Entree Blooms With Brief Recipes

AS WARM, mild weather beckons you and your family outdoors, even those who love to cook may not want to spend a lot of time making a meal. At times like that, you need a tasty menu you can pull together in just a matter of minutes!

The appealing meal here is made up of family-tested and -approved recipes from three time-conscious cooks. You can have everything ready to serve in about 30 minutes.

Special Pork Chops from LaDane Wilson have zesty flair and are a snap to prepare. "I work 9 hours a day, so I need delicious and simple recipes like this one," shares this Alexander City, Alabama cook. "My husband thinks I work hard fixing meals, but these chops are good and easy. In summer, I can my own salsa and use some to top these chops."

Golden Potatoes make even canned potatoes taste terrific. The cheesy seasoning creates a puffy golden coating, making these an attractive addition to the table. This fancy-looking side dish comes from Carla Cagle of Marceline, Missouri.

Broccoli-Mushroom Medley is a fresh flavorful vegetable dish shared by Cherie Sechrist of Red Lion, Pennsylvania. "People will think you fussed when you offer this elegant skillet side dish," Cherie says.

Special Pork Chops

6 to 8 boneless pork loin chops (1/3 inch thick)
1 tablespoon vegetable oil
1 jar (16 ounces) salsa

In an ovenproof skillet, brown the pork chops in oil; drain. Pour salsa over chops. Bake, uncovered, at 350° for 25 minutes or until pork juices run clear. **Yield:** 4-6 servings.

Golden Potatoes

2 cans (16 ounces *each*) whole white potatoes, drained
1/4 cup butter *or* margarine, melted
1/2 teaspoon seasoned salt
2 to 3 tablespoons grated Parmesan cheese
1 tablespoon minced fresh parsley

Place potatoes in an ungreased 8-in. square baking dish. Pour butter over potatoes. Sprinkle with seasoned salt, cheese and parsley. Bake, uncovered, at 350° for 25 minutes or until lightly browned. **Yield:** 4-6 servings.

Broccoli-Mushroom Medley

☑ Uses less fat, sugar or salt. Includes Nutritional Analysis and Diabetic Exchanges.

1-1/2 pounds fresh broccoli, cut into florets
1 teaspoon lemon juice
1 teaspoon salt, optional
1 teaspoon sugar
1 teaspoon cornstarch
1/4 teaspoon ground nutmeg
1 cup sliced fresh mushrooms
1 medium onion, sliced into rings
1 to 2 garlic cloves, minced
3 tablespoons vegetable oil

Steam broccoli for 1-2 minutes or until crisp-tender. Rinse in cold water and set aside. In a bowl, combine lemon juice, salt if desired, sugar, cornstarch and nutmeg; set aside. In a large skillet or wok over high heat, stir-fry mushrooms, onion and garlic in oil for 3 minutes. Add broccoli and lemon juice mixture; stir-fry for 1-2 minutes. Serve immediately. **Yield:** 6 servings. **Nutritional Analysis:** One serving (prepared without salt) equals 88 calories, 22 mg sodium, 0 cholesterol, 10 gm carbohydrate, 4 gm protein, 5 gm fat. **Diabetic Exchanges:** 2 vegetable, 1 fat.

Bushel of Broccoli Tips

To select good broccoli, look for tight compact bud clusters with uniform dark green or purplish color. The stems should be tender, slightly moist and lighter green than the buds. Avoid clusters with soft or slippery spots.

For optimum flavor and nutrition, wash broccoli but don't soak it in water. Use fresh broccoli as soon as possible. To cook broccoli, use just a bit of water and a short cooking time for the best results.

Easy Easter Entree

HOLIDAYS are a wonderful time to get together with family and friends to share a meal, and Easter's no exception. But when hectic weekdays and weekends keep you hopping, you'll reach for these mouth-watering recipes often.

Apricot Ham Steak turns leftover Easter ham into a wonderfully different main course. And for an easy alternative to the apricot glaze in this recipe, see the tip at the bottom of page 29.

Hot-off-the-griddle Potato Pancakes and some garden-fresh green beans really round out the springtime meal. For dessert, there's nothing better than a deliciously creamy Easy Rice Pudding. The recipes were created by the *Taste of Home* Test Kitchen.

Apricot Ham Steak

Ham is a versatile main menu item that's a standby with all country cooks. One of the best and easiest ways to serve ham slices is topped off with a slightly sweet glaze, like this apricot version.

> 4 slices fully cooked ham (1/2 inch thick)
> 2 tablespoons butter *or* margarine, *divided*
> 1/2 cup apricot preserves
> 1 tablespoon cider vinegar
> 1/4 teaspoon ground ginger
Dash salt
Hot cooked green beans, optional

In a skillet, saute ham slices in 1 tablespoon of butter until lightly browned, turning once. Meanwhile, in a saucepan or microwave-safe bowl, combine the preserves, vinegar, ginger, salt and remaining butter; heat through. Serve ham with the apricot sauce and green beans if desired. **Yield:** 4 servings.

Potato Pancakes

Preparing traditional potato pancakes can be time-consuming…so you'll relish this recipe. That's because there's no need to grate potatoes. By using frozen hash browns, these "spud-tacular" pancakes are ready in a hurry!

> 4 cups frozen shredded hash browns
> 1/2 cup finely chopped onion

> 1/4 cup minced fresh parsley
> 2 tablespoons milk
> 2 eggs, beaten
> 1/4 cup all-purpose flour
> 1 teaspoon salt
Vegetable oil

Place hash browns in a strainer and rinse with cold water until thawed. Drain thoroughly; transfer to a large bowl. Add onion, parsley, milk, eggs, flour and salt; mix well. In a skillet over medium heat, heat 1/4 in. of oil. Drop batter by 1/4 cupfuls into hot oil. Fry until golden brown on both sides. Drain on paper towels. **Yield:** 4 servings.

Easy Rice Pudding

Rice pudding has been a family favorite for generations, both because of its fantastic flavor and ease of preparation. Your family will love this pudding's creamy texture, and you will love its fast-to-fix convenience.

    4 cups milk
    1 package (3 ounces) cook-and-serve
      vanilla pudding mix
    1 cup instant rice
    1 egg, beaten
    1/4 teaspoon ground cinnamon
    1/4 teaspoon vanilla extract

In a saucepan, combine the first five ingredients; bring to a full boil, stirring constantly. Remove from the heat and stir in vanilla. Cool for 5 minutes, stirring twice. Spoon into individual serving dishes. Serve warm or chill until serving. **Yield:** 4 servings.

Likable Leftovers

If you're looking for an easy glaze to keep on hand, small amounts of jelly left in jars can be combined, melted and used as a glaze for ham.

Harvest of Goodness

YOU'VE WORKED HARD in your garden all summer, and now it's time to reap the rewards with a bountiful dinner. Herbs and fresh peppers add a palate-pleasing touch to Chunky Spaghetti Sauce. Your family will never tire of zucchini when they sample Zesty Zucchini. Then cool off with a slice of Refreshing Lemon Pie and a glass of iced tea.

Chunky Spaghetti Sauce

When your hungry clan requests, "Spaghetti, please!", you'll be happy to oblige with this simple savory sauce. It proves appetizingly that homemade spaghetti sauce doesn't have to simmer all day in order to be hearty and delicious.

       1 pound bulk Italian sausage
       1 to 2 medium green peppers, julienned
    1/2 medium onion, chopped
       1 garlic clove, minced
       2 cans (14-1/2 ounces *each*) Italian stewed
           tomatoes
    1/4 cup tomato paste
    1-1/2 teaspoons minced fresh oregano *or* 1/2
           teaspoon dried oregano
    1-1/2 teaspoons minced fresh basil *or* 1/2
           teaspoon dried basil
    Hot cooked pasta

Brown sausage in a large saucepan; drain. Add green peppers, onion and garlic; cook until tender, about 5 minutes. Add tomatoes, tomato paste, oregano and basil; simmer, uncovered, for 10-15 minutes. Serve over pasta. **Yield:** 4 servings.

Zesty Zucchini

Here's a great way to use up an often overabundant vegetable. Perfect for potlucks and everyday dinners, it's sure to become a recipe you reach for frequently.

    1/3 cup vegetable oil
    1/4 cup cider *or* white wine vinegar
       1 tablespoon minced fresh basil *or* 1
           teaspoon dried basil
    1/2 teaspoon salt
    1/4 teaspoon pepper
    1/4 teaspoon garlic powder
       2 to 3 medium zucchini, sliced

In a large bowl, whisk together the first six ingredients. Add zucchini and toss. Chill until serving. **Yield:** 4 servings.

Refreshing Lemon Pie

Have little time on your hands, but your family still expects dessert with dinner? This easy-as-pie recipe pro-

vides a refreshingly simple solution. You'll appreciate the short list of ingredients—and the even shorter preparation time! Your family will love the cool lemony flavor of this pie.

> 1 can (14 ounces) sweetened condensed milk
> 1/2 cup lemon juice
> 1 tablespoon grated lemon peel
> 2 to 3 drops yellow food coloring, optional
> 1 carton (8 ounces) frozen whipped topping, thawed
> 1 graham cracker crust (9 inches)

Mint leaves and lemon peel strips, optional

In a bowl, combine milk, lemon juice, grated lemon peel and food coloring if desired; mix until smooth (mixture will begin to thicken). Fold in whipped topping; spoon into crust. Chill until serving. If desired, garnish with mint leaves and lemon peel strips. Refrigerate leftovers. **Yield:** 6-8 servings.

A Zest for Lemons

Lemon zest is the outer peel or rind of the lemon. To remove it, peel thin strips with a small sharp knife, being careful not to include the white membrane, and mince firmly.

Spring Supper Bursting With Flavor

CELEBRATE the arrival of spring by gathering family and friends for this pleasing pork chop dinner. Everything can be prepared in under half an hour, leaving you more time to spend with your guests.

A tempting and beautiful glaze makes Mustard-Apricot Pork Chops an impressive main dish that looks like you fussed over it. "This recipe is so easy and so good," says Sheila Townsend of West Des Moines, Iowa. These tender chops are nice to serve during the week as well as for company on weekends.

Asparagus with Almonds will please the palates of everyone—even those who generally don't care for asparagus, assures Eileen Bechtel of Wainwright, Alberta. "I look forward to spring each year so I can make this tasty side dish."

Fruit Parfaits are a refreshing fruity treat, and you can use whatever flavor of gelatin you like. Spring City, Tennessee cook Erlene Cornelius shares the recipe. And because it calls for canned fruit, you can rely on it as a tasty dessert any time of year.

Mustard-Apricot Pork Chops

1/3 cup apricot preserves
2 tablespoons Dijon mustard
4 pork loin chops (1/2 to 3/4 inch thick)
3 green onions, chopped
Hot cooked rice

In a small saucepan over low heat, cook and stir preserves and mustard until preserves are melted; set aside. Place pork chops on a lightly greased broiler pan; broil 4 in. from the heat for 5 minutes. Brush with half of the glaze; turn pork chops. Broil 5 minutes longer; brush with the remaining glaze. Broil 2-4 minutes more or until meat juices run clear. Top with onions. Serve over rice. **Yield:** 4 servings.

Asparagus with Almonds

2 tablespoons sliced almonds
4 teaspoons olive *or* vegetable oil, *divided*
1 pound fresh asparagus, cut into 2-inch pieces
1/4 cup water
1 teaspoon sugar
1/4 teaspoon salt
Dash pepper
1 teaspoon lemon juice

In a skillet, saute almonds in 1 teaspoon of oil until lightly browned; remove and set aside. In the same skillet, saute asparagus in the remaining oil for 1 minute. Add water, sugar, salt and pepper; bring to a boil. Reduce heat; cover and simmer for 3-4 minutes or until asparagus is tender. Drain. Sprinkle with lemon juice; top with almonds. **Yield:** 3-4 servings.

Fruit Parfaits

✓ Uses less fat, sugar or salt. Includes Nutritional Analysis and Diabetic Exchanges.

1 can (15 ounces) fruit cocktail
1 package (3 ounces) lemon gelatin
8 ice cubes (1-1/2 cups crushed ice)

Drain fruit cocktail, reserving the syrup. Divide fruit among four parfait glasses and set aside. Add water to the syrup to measure 3/4 cup; pour into a saucepan. Bring to a boil. Place the gelatin in a blender; carefully add syrup. Cover and blend on low until gelatin is dissolved, about 30 seconds. Add ice; cover and blend until dissolved, about 1 minute. Pour over the fruit. Cover and refrigerate until set, about 15 minutes. **Yield:** 4 servings. **Nutritional Analysis:** One 1/2-cup serving (prepared with fruit cocktail in light syrup and sugar-free gelatin) equals 69 calories, 53 mg sodium, 0 cholesterol, 16 gm carbohydrate, 1 gm protein, trace fat. **Diabetic Exchange:** 1 fruit.

Asparagus Tips

You can store unwashed asparagus in a sealed plastic bag in the refrigerator for up to 4 days. Just before using, cut off the tough white portion on the stalk and soak in cold water to clean.

Stir-Fry Is Simple Way To Serve Supper

AFTER SPRING has "sprung" where you live, you can't wait to start enjoying the flavors of the season. There's no better way to do that than by serving foods that feature plenty of refreshing, colorful produce.

Here three country cooks share family-favorite recipes for delightful dishes showcasing peppers, peas and pineapple! Together, these foods create a complete-meal menu that goes from start to serving in 30 minutes or less.

With peppers, onion and celery, Curried Beef Stir-Fry is a flavorful eye-catching entree. "I created this hearty recipe myself and prepare it often when time is short," says Karen Munn from St. Francois Xavier, Manitoba.

Dilly Pea Salad dresses up peas in a deliciously different way. "I got the recipe for this refreshing salad from my best friend when I was a young bride," shares Rita Applegate of La Mesa, California. "I've shared it with many people over the years."

Broiled Pineapple Dessert is a sweet and tangy treat that looks impressive but is very little fuss, assures Karen Owen of Rising Sun, Indiana. "Folks frequently request seconds of this fruity dessert."

Curried Beef Stir-Fry

- 3 **tablespoons soy sauce**
- 3 **garlic cloves, minced**
- 1 **tablespoon minced fresh gingerroot** *or*
  1 teaspoon ground ginger
- 4 **tablespoons vegetable oil,** *divided*
- 1 **pound boneless sirloin steak, cut into**
  1/8-inch strips
- 1 **large onion, cut into 1-inch pieces**
- 1 **medium green pepper, cut into 1-inch**
  pieces
- 1 **medium sweet red pepper, cut into 1-inch**
  pieces
- 2 **large celery ribs, sliced**
- 1 **cup cold water**
- 5 **teaspoons cornstarch**
- 1 **to 2 teaspoons curry powder**

Hot cooked rice *or* **noodles**

In a bowl, combine soy sauce, garlic, ginger and 2 tablespoons oil. Add beef; toss to coat. Cover and refrigerate for 15-20 minutes. In a large skillet or wok, heat remaining oil. Stir-fry beef over medium-high heat for 2-3 minutes. Remove beef and set aside. In the same skillet, stir-fry onion for 1 minute; add peppers and celery. Stir-fry for 2 minutes; return beef to the skillet. Combine water, cornstarch and curry until smooth; add to skillet. Bring to a boil and boil for 1 minute, stirring constantly. Serve over rice or noodles. **Yield:** 4 servings.

Dilly Pea Salad

☑ Uses less fat, sugar or salt. Includes Nutritional Analysis and Diabetic Exchanges.

- 1 **cup (8 ounces) sour cream**
- 4 **teaspoons lemon juice**
- 4 **teaspoons sliced green onion**
- 2 **teaspoons sugar**
- 1 **teaspoon dill weed**
- 1/2 **teaspoon curry powder**
- 1/2 **teaspoon salt, optional**
- 1/4 **teaspoon pepper**
- 2 **packages (10 ounces** *each***) frozen peas,**
  thawed

In a medium bowl, combine the first eight ingredients. Add peas; toss. Chill until serving. **Yield:** 6 servings. **Nutritional Analysis:** One 1/2-cup serving (prepared with nonfat sour cream and without salt) equals 123 calories, 111 mg sodium, 3 mg cholesterol, 23 gm carbohydrate, 7 gm protein, trace fat. **Diabetic Exchange:** 1-1/2 starch.

Broiled Pineapple Dessert

- 4 **pineapple slices**
- 8 **teaspoons brown sugar**
- 2 **tablespoons butter** *or* **margarine**
- 4 **slices pound cake**
- 4 **scoops vanilla ice cream**

Ground cinnamon

Place pineapple slices on a broiler pan. Top each with 2 teaspoons brown sugar and 1-1/2 teaspoons butter. Broil 4 in. from the heat for 3-5 minutes or until the sugar is bubbly. Place each slice on a piece of pound cake; top with ice cream and sprinkle with cinnamon. Serve immediately. **Yield:** 4 servings.

New Year Cheer

WHAT BETTER WAY to greet Father Time than with this fantastic feast? A robust mushroom-onion sauce enhances the flavor of specially seasoned Herbed Sirloin. You'll agree the cheesy Easy Au Gratin Potatoes go perfectly with all your favorite main meals. And for the time being, you'll want to toss aside those New Year resolutions and relish every bite of Raspberry Chocolate Trifle!

Herbed Sirloin

There's no reason to head outdoors to serve up sizzling steak. One skillet's all you need to brown the meat, cook the vegetables and make the accompanying marvelous mustard sauce. With such fantastic flavor, you just may prepare steak this way no matter what time of year!

1-1/2 to 2 pounds boneless top sirloin (1 inch thick)
  2 tablespoons vegetable oil
  1 small onion, sliced
  2 cups sliced fresh mushrooms
1/2 cup beef broth
  2 teaspoons Dijon mustard
  1 teaspoon Worcestershire sauce
1/2 teaspoon dried thyme
1/4 teaspoon garlic powder

Cut steak into four serving-size pieces; brown in a large skillet in oil for 5 minutes on each side. Add onion and mushrooms. Cook until vegetables are tender and the meat has reached desired doneness, stirring occasionally. Remove meat to a platter and keep warm. Combine the broth, mustard, Worcestershire sauce, thyme and garlic powder; stir into vegetables. Bring to a boil. Reduce heat; simmer for 2-3 minutes. Spoon over meat. **Yield:** 4 servings.

Easy Au Gratin Potatoes

One taste of this classic dish and you'll never buy a store-bought box of au gratin potatoes again! Thinly sliced "spuds" cook up tender in no time. Your family will request this recipe many times over.

3/4 cup half-and-half cream
1/2 cup milk
1/2 teaspoon salt
1/4 teaspoon garlic powder
  3 medium potatoes, peeled and thinly sliced
  1 cup seasoned salad croutons, *divided*
1/8 teaspoon pepper
1/2 cup shredded cheddar cheese

In a medium saucepan, bring cream, milk, salt and garlic powder to a boil. Add potatoes; reduce heat. Cover and simmer for 10-15 minutes or until the potatoes are tender. Coarsely crush 1/4 cup of croutons. Remove potatoes from the heat; stir in the crushed croutons and pepper. Pour into a greased 1-1/2-qt. baking dish. Sprinkle with the cheese and remaining croutons. Bake, uncovered, at 400° for 5-6 minutes or until the cheese is melted. **Yield:** 4 servings.

Raspberry Chocolate Trifle

"Elegant but easy" perfectly describes this rich and creamy trifle. Prepared pound cake, frozen berries and instant pudding combine to create one mouth-watering masterpiece that is great for both weekday dinners or special-occasion suppers. For a little variety, substitute angel food cake or another variety of fruit and preserves.

- **2 cups cold milk**
- **1 package (3.9 ounces) instant chocolate pudding mix**
- **1 loaf (10-3/4 ounces) frozen pound cake, thawed**
- **2 cups fresh *or* frozen raspberries, thawed**
- **1 cup raspberry preserves**
- **Whipped topping**
- **Additional raspberries, optional**

Mix milk and pudding mix according to package directions; chill. Cut cake into 1-in. cubes; place half in a 2-qt. glass bowl. Gently stir together raspberries and preserves; spoon half over cake. Pour half of the pudding over raspberries. Cover with remaining cake cubes. Layer with remaining berries and pudding. Chill until serving. Garnish with whipped topping and raspberries if desired. **Yield:** 4-6 servings.

Savory Skillet Supper That's Ready in a Snap

WHEN COOLER DAYS signal the start of the busy pre-holiday season, even dedicated cooks can't always spend much time in the kitchen.

That's when speedy supper solutions like this come in handy.

Sausage Skillet Supper is a simple and satisfying main dish and a favorite of Mildred Sherrer's family in Bay City, Texas.

Honey Poppy Seed Dressing, sent by Michelle Bentley of Niceville, Florida, is a light, refreshing way to dress up a plain lettuce salad.

Lemon Garlic Bread has a deliciously different hint of lemon. Adeline Piscitelli of Sayreville, New Jersey shares the recipe.

Speedy Rice Pudding has rich, old-fashioned flavor, but it's quick to make, assures great-grandmother Ann Vershowske of West Allis, Wisconsin.

Sausage Skillet Supper

1 pound bulk pork sausage
1 can (14-1/2 ounces) stewed tomatoes, undrained
1 can (16 ounces) kidney beans, rinsed and drained
1 cup uncooked long grain rice
1 cup water
2/3 cup picante sauce *or* salsa

In a medium skillet, cook and crumble sausage; drain. Add remaining ingredients; bring to a boil. Reduce heat; cover and simmer for 20-25 minutes or until rice is tender. **Yield:** 6-8 servings.

Honey Poppy Seed Dressing

1/3 cup vegetable oil
1/4 cup honey
2 tablespoons cider vinegar
2 teaspoons poppy seeds
1/2 teaspoon salt

In a small bowl or jar with tight-fitting lid, combine all ingredients; mix or shake well. Serve over a green salad or fresh fruit. Store in the refrigerator. **Yield:** about 2/3 cup.

Lemon Garlic Bread

1 loaf (1 pound) French bread
1/2 cup butter *or* margarine, melted
2 tablespoons grated Parmesan cheese
4 teaspoons lemon juice
1 tablespoon grated lemon peel
1 garlic clove, minced
1/4 teaspoon pepper

Cut bread diagonally into 1-in. slices. Combine remaining ingredients; brush over cut sides of bread. Wrap loaf in foil. Bake at 400° for 15-20 minutes or until heated through. **Yield:** 8-10 servings.

Speedy Rice Pudding

4 cups milk
1 egg, beaten
1 package (3 ounces) cook-and-serve vanilla pudding mix
1 cup uncooked instant rice
1/4 cup raisins
1/4 teaspoon ground cinnamon
1/8 teaspoon ground nutmeg

In a saucepan, combine milk, egg and pudding mix. Add rice and raisins. Bring to a boil over medium heat, stirring constantly. Remove from the heat; cool for 5 minutes, stirring twice. Pour into dessert dishes or a serving bowl. Serve immediately or cover with plastic wrap and refrigerate. Sprinkle with cinnamon and nutmeg. **Yield:** 8-10 servings.

Eggspert Advice

If a recipe calls for eggs to be at room temperature before mixing with other ingredients, remove the eggs from the refrigerator no more than 30 minutes before using to avoid bacteria growth.

Leprechaun's Lunch

EVEN EYES that aren't Irish will be smiling when they behold this bountiful meal. Corned Beef and Cabbage Sandwiches tastefully combine creamy cabbage and tender corned beef. And folks will be delighted to see a bit o' the green when you serve them some hearty Spinach Potato Soup. Extra-easy Shamrock Sundaes—with mint ice cream and homemade chocolate sauce—and a refreshing beverage top off the meal tastily.

Corned Beef and Cabbage Sandwiches

You don't have to wait for St. Patrick's Day to serve these festive sandwiches. Your family is sure to enjoy the flavorful combination of cabbage and corned beef piled high on a hard roll any time of year.

- 1/3 cup mayonnaise
- 1 tablespoon vinegar
- 1/4 teaspoon ground mustard
- 1/4 teaspoon celery seed
- 1/4 teaspoon pepper
- 1-1/2 cups thinly shredded raw cabbage
- 4 kaiser *or* hard rolls, split
- 3/4 to 1 pound fully cooked corned beef, sliced

In a bowl, combine mayonnaise, vinegar, mustard, celery seed and pepper until smooth. Stir in cabbage and mix well. Spoon onto the bottom halves of rolls. Cover with corned beef; replace tops of rolls. Serve immediately. **Yield:** 4 servings.

Some Souper Storage Ideas

Before freezing homemade soup, refrigerate it until the fat rises to the surface. Skim off the fat and discard any bones.

To store individual servings from a big batch of soup, line several bowls with plastic wrap, pour in the soup and freeze. Once frozen, the soup can be popped out of the bowls and stored in large freezer bags. This also makes a nice gift for an ill friend or someone living alone.

Spinach Potato Soup

When your clan is hungry, hot and hearty soup surely fills the bill...not to mention stomachs! You'll find the spinach in this recipe makes this soup more colorful than ordinary potato soup.

- 2 cups cubed peeled potatoes (1/2-inch pieces)
- 1-1/2 cups water
- 1 tablespoon dried minced onion
- 1 teaspoon instant chicken bouillon granules
- 1/2 teaspoon garlic salt
- 1 cup thinly sliced fresh *or* chopped frozen spinach

1 cup whipping cream
1/4 teaspoon ground nutmeg

In a saucepan, combine the potatoes, water, onion and bouillon; bring to a boil. Cook until potatoes are tender, about 10 minutes. Add the remaining ingredients and cook until spinach is tender and heated through. **Yield:** 4 servings.

—— ∽∞⋅⋚⋙ ——

Shamrock Sundaes

If your family loves ice cream (and whose doesn't?), you'll probably serve these simple-to-make sun-daes—with their from-scratch chocolate sauce—often.

1/4 cup butter *or* margarine
1 square (1 ounce) unsweetened chocolate
1 cup sugar
1/3 cup half-and-half cream
1/4 cup corn syrup
1/2 teaspoon vanilla extract
Mint ice cream

In a saucepan, melt butter and chocolate over low heat. Add sugar, cream and corn syrup; bring to a boil, stirring constantly. Boil for 1 minute. Remove from the heat and stir in vanilla. Serve warm or cool over ice cream. **Yield:** about 1-2/3 cups chocolate sauce.

Reel in Raves on Warm Sunny Days

ARE YOU FISHING for fast and fun foods to prepare for your famished family on hurried, hectic days? You'll love this quick and easy meal, while everyone will agree it's "reel"-y delicious!

Don't settle for ordinary hamburgers when you can serve Zesty Salmon Burgers. "They're easy to make and are a regular summer main dish at our house," reports Melanie Dunn of Wilmore, Kansas. "Horseradish adds a tasty zip to convenient canned salmon." Even those people who normally don't care for salmon will likely be "hooked" after one bite of these specialty fish sandwiches.

With water chestnuts and celery, Crunchy Pea Salad is a refreshing side dish with a fun crunch. "Frozen peas are a handy base for this good-tasting salad," remarks Mary Reid Fisher of Brownwood, Texas. "It's also a great dish for a potluck because it can be made ahead. Everyone enjoys this when I serve it."

If you're watching your waistline, cut some of the calories and fat by simply substituting fat-free mayonnaise and nonfat sour cream.

Lemon Crisp Cookies are a snap to make using a convenient boxed cake mix. Says Julia Livingston from Frostproof, Florida, "The sunny yellow color and big lemon flavor are sure to bring a bunch of smiles." You'll likely prepare these tempting treats even when you do have time to bake.

If you have a yellow cake mix on your pantry shelf that you'd like to use up, feel free to use it in place of the lemon cake mix. The cookies won't have a strong lemon flavor, but they'll still be delicious!

Zesty Salmon Burgers

      1 can (14-3/4 ounces) salmon, drained, skin and bones removed
      2 eggs
  1/2 cup dry bread crumbs
  1/4 cup finely chopped onion
  1/4 cup mayonnaise
      1 to 2 tablespoons prepared horseradish
      1 tablespoon diced pimientos, optional
  1/4 teaspoon salt
  1/8 teaspoon pepper
      2 tablespoons butter *or* margarine
      4 kaiser rolls, split
Lettuce leaves

Combine the first nine ingredients; mix well. Shape into four patties. In a skillet over medium heat, cook patties in butter until browned, about 6 minutes on each side. Serve on rolls with lettuce. **Yield:** 4 servings.

Crunchy Pea Salad

☑ Uses less fat, sugar or salt. Includes Nutritional Analysis and Diabetic Exchanges.

      1 package (10 ounces) frozen peas, thawed
      1 can (8 ounces) sliced water chestnuts, drained
      1 cup thinly sliced celery
  1/2 cup sliced green onions
  1/4 cup mayonnaise
  1/4 cup sour cream
  1/2 teaspoon seasoned salt, optional

In a bowl, combine the first four ingredients. In a small bowl, combine mayonnaise, sour cream and seasoned salt if desired; mix well. Add to the pea mixture; toss to coat. Chill until serving. **Yield:** 8 servings. **Nutritional Analysis:** One 1/2-cup serving (prepared with fat-free mayonnaise and nonfat sour cream and without seasoned salt) equals 60 calories, 116 mg sodium, 1 mg cholesterol, 12 gm carbohydrate, 3 gm protein, trace fat. **Diabetic Exchange:** 1 starch.

Lemon Crisp Cookies

      1 package (18-1/4 ounces) lemon cake mix
      1 cup crisp rice cereal
  1/2 cup butter *or* margarine, melted
      1 egg, beaten
      1 teaspoon grated lemon peel

In a large bowl, combine all ingredients until well mixed (dough will be crumbly). Shape into 1-in. balls. Place 2 in. apart on ungreased baking sheets. Bake at 350° for 10-12 minutes or until set. Cool for 1 minute; remove from pan to a wire rack to cool completely. **Yield:** about 4 dozen.

Give Plain Spa[ghetti] Dinner a Tasty T[wist]

THINK YOU CAN'T serve your family a wholesome meal with an Italian twist because time in the kitchen is often too short? Put away that jar of prepared spaghetti sauce and think again!

It's easy to offer a homemade meal in minutes with the three delicious dishes featured here. In fact, this quick menu goes from start to finish in less than 30 minutes!

Spaghetti with Sausage and Peppers comes from Ginger Harrell of El Dorado, Arkansas. "Smoked turkey sausage is a wonderful change of pace from traditional Italian sausage and ground beef sauces," relates Ginger. "And with fresh peppers and onion, this dish is not only quick, but economical, too."

While you likely don't have time to make bread from scratch on hurried days, you can dress up fresh store-bought bread in a jiffy with a few simple ingredients. "Slices of delicious Poppy Seed French Bread bake up crisp with a poppy seed and Parmesan cheese coating," informs Leavenworth, Washington cook Ruth Andrewson, who shares the recipe.

Strawberry Delight from Lyons, Georgia's Suzanne McKinely is a cool and creamy dessert that gets a head start with a purchased graham cracker crust.

"I often substitute other berries," Suzanne shares. "You can also use different pudding flavors."

Spaghetti with Sausage and Peppers

    1 pound smoked turkey sausage, cut into 1/4-inch slices
    2 medium green peppers, thinly sliced
    2 medium sweet red peppers, thinly sliced
    1 medium onion, halved and thinly sliced
    2 cans (14-1/2 ounces *each*) diced tomatoes, undrained
    3 garlic cloves, minced
    6 to 8 drops hot pepper sauce
    1 teaspoon paprika
 1/2 teaspoon salt
 1/4 teaspoon cayenne pepper
 1/2 cup chicken broth
    2 tablespoons cornstarch
    1 package (12 ounces) spaghetti, cooked and drained

In a Dutch oven, brown sausage. Add peppers and onion; saute for 2 minutes. Add tomatoes, garlic, hot pepper sauce, pap[rika and cayenne] pepper; cook and stir until the[peppers are ten]-der. Combine broth and cornstar[ch; stir into sausage] mixture. Bring to a boil. Cook and [stir until thick]-ened. Add spaghetti; cook for 5 min[utes, stirring] occasionally. **Yield:** 6-8 servings.

Poppy Seed French Bread

 1/4 cup butter *or* margarine, softened
 1/2 cup grated Parmesan cheese
1-1/2 tablespoons poppy seeds
    8 slices French bread (1 inch thick)

Combine butter, Parmesan cheese and poppy seeds; spread on both sides of each piece of bread. Place on a baking sheet. Bake at 350° for 12-16 minutes, turning once. **Yield:** 6-8 servings.

Strawberry Delight

    2 cups frozen whole strawberries, thawed
Red food coloring, optional
    1 package (3.4 ounces) instant vanilla pudding mix
    1 carton (12 ounces) frozen whipped topping, thawed
    1 graham cracker crust (9 inches)
 1/2 cup flaked coconut, toasted

In a mixing bowl, crush strawberries. Add food coloring if desired. Beat in pudding mix until smooth. Fold in whipped topping. Pour into crust; sprinkle with coconut. Chill until serving. Store leftovers in the refrigerator. **Yield:** 6-8 servings.

Toasting Coconut

Recipes often call for toasted coconut. To prepare, spread the flaked coconut on a baking sheet and bake at 350° until light golden brown, stirring often. Timing will depend on how finely the coconut is shredded and the weight of your baking pan. Generally coconut will toast in 6-10 minutes, but keep a close watch to prevent burning.

ghetti
Twist

...rika, salt and cayenne ...vegetables are ten-...h; add to sausage ...stir until thick-...utes, stirring

Sweetheart Pancakes

Hot-off-the-griddle goodies are always a welcome sight on the table...morning, noon and night. Instead of serving these palate-pleasing pancakes with ordinary maple syrup, make this extraordinary cherry sauce. You'll be thanked mmm-many times over!

1-3/4 **cups all-purpose flour**
   2 **tablespoons sugar**
   2 **teaspoons baking powder**
1/2 **teaspoon salt**
   2 **eggs**
1-1/2 **cups milk**
   3 **tablespoons vegetable oil**
1/2 **teaspoon lemon juice**
CHERRY SAUCE:
   1 **can (21 ounces) cherry pie filling**
1/2 to 3/4 **teaspoon almond extract**
1/8 to 1/4 **teaspoon ground nutmeg**
Whipped cream in a can

In a bowl, combine the flour, sugar, baking powder and salt. In another bowl, beat the eggs; add milk, oil and lemon juice. Stir into dry ingredients just until moistened. Pour batter by 1/3 cupfuls onto a lightly greased hot griddle; turn when bubbles form on top of pancakes. Cook until the second side is golden brown. For cherry sauce, combine pie filling, extract and nutmeg in a medium saucepan. Cook, stirring occasionally, until heated through. To serve as shown in the photo, stack pancakes on serving plates and make a heart outline with whipped cream; spoon cherry sauce into heart. **Yield:** 4 servings (12 pancakes).

Sausage Granola Squares

No morning meal would be complete without a meaty side dish. With a trio of ingredients, these homemade sausage squares couldn't be easier...or more down-home delicious. Plus, they're oven-baked instead of pan-fried, for less mess and greater convenience.

1/2 **pound bulk pork sausage**
3/4 **cup granola cereal with fruit and nuts**
   1 **egg, lightly beaten**

Combine all ingredients; pat into a greased shallow 2-cup baking dish. Bake, uncovered, at 375° for 20 minutes or until browned. **Yield:** 4 servings.

Morning Fruit Shake

In addition to offering an assortment of juices and milk, why not serve this cool beverage filled with your family's favorite fruit flavors? Your thirsty clan will savor it so much, you'll be asked to make it from sunrise to sundown!

✓ Uses less fat, sugar or salt. Includes Nutritional Analysis and Diabetic Exchanges.

1 cup cranberry juice
2 medium ripe bananas, sliced

2 cartons (8 ounces *each*) raspberry yogurt *or* flavor of choice
1 tablespoon confectioners' sugar, optional
Few drops red food coloring, optional
Mint leaves, optional

In a blender, combine first five ingredients; blend at medium speed until smooth. Garnish with mint if desired. Serve immediately. **Yield:** 4 servings. **Nutritional Analysis:** One 3/4-cup serving (prepared with sugar-free raspberry yogurt and without confectioners' sugar) equals 138 calories, 64 mg sodium, 0 cholesterol, 30 gm carbohydrate, 6 gm protein, trace fat. **Diabetic Exchanges:** 1 fruit, 1 skim milk.

Quick Cooking Will Keep Your Summer Kitchen Cool

WHEN THE KITCHEN heats up before you even turn on the oven, cooking with the microwave and outside on the grill is a wonderful way to keep your cool…and make a quick meal.

Meat Loaf Hamburgers are tender, mellow-tasting burgers everyone will enjoy, assures Sandi Pichon of Slidell, Louisiana. "They're a nice alternative to plain ground beef patties and very popular whenever I serve them," she says.

Microwave German Potato Salad has big flavor for a quick salad. "The first time I tried this easy side dish I was so impressed I had to have the recipe," recalls Barbara Erdmann of West Allis, Wisconsin. "That's what happens to most people who taste it. It's a time-saver when I need a crowd-pleasing salad for a get-together."

Fruit-Topped Almond Cream is a light and refreshing dessert. The recipe comes from Donna Friedrich of Fishkill, New York. "It's delicious with berries, but it can be made all year using whatever fruit is available," Donna informs.

Meat Loaf Hamburgers

    1 cup (8 ounces) sour cream
1-1/4 cups crushed cornflakes
    1 tablespoon diced onion
   1/2 to 1 teaspoon salt
   1/8 teaspoon pepper
1-1/2 pounds ground beef
    8 kaiser *or* hamburger buns, split
Lettuce leaves
Tomato slices

In a large bowl, combine the first five ingredients; add beef and mix well. Shape into eight patties. Grill, broil or pan-fry until the meat is no longer pink. Serve on buns with lettuce and tomato. **Yield:** 8 servings.

Hamburger Helper

Don't press hamburger patties with a spatula or other utensil while pan-frying them—this squeezes out the meat's flavorful juices.

Microwave German Potato Salad

    2 pounds red potatoes, cooked and sliced
    3 hard-cooked eggs, chopped
  1/2 cup chopped onion
  1/2 cup chopped celery
    6 bacon strips, diced
    2 tablespoons sugar
    4 teaspoons all-purpose flour
    2 tablespoons vinegar
  1/2 teaspoon salt
  1/8 teaspoon pepper
  3/4 cup milk

In a large bowl, combine potatoes, eggs, onion and celery; set aside. Place the bacon in a microwave-safe bowl; cover with a paper towel and microwave on high for 2 minutes. Stir. Microwave 3-4 minutes longer or until the bacon is crisp, stirring after each minute. Remove bacon to paper towel to drain; reserve 2 tablespoons drippings. Stir sugar, flour, vinegar, salt and pepper into drippings until smooth; gradually add milk. Microwave on high for 5-6 minutes, stirring every 2 minutes, or until thickened. Pour over potato mixture; toss. Top with bacon. Serve immediately. **Yield:** 8 servings. **Editor's Note:** This recipe was tested in a 700-watt microwave.

Fruit-Topped Almond Cream

2-1/2 cups cold milk
    1 package (3.4 ounces) instant French vanilla pudding mix
    1 cup whipping cream
  1/2 to 3/4 teaspoon almond extract
    3 cups assorted fruit (strawberries, grapes, raspberries, blueberries, mandarin oranges)

In a large mixing bowl, combine milk and pudding mix. Beat on low speed for 2 minutes; set aside. In a small mixing bowl, beat cream and extract until stiff peaks form. Fold into the pudding. Spoon into a shallow 2-qt. serving dish. Chill. Top with fruit just before serving. **Yield:** 8 servings.

Dig into Delicious Outdoor Dinner

WARM SUMMER DAYS are made to be spent outdoors, so why waste hours in the kitchen when you can make this speedy and satisfying supper and head back outside? Each dish is easy to make and can be ready in under 30 minutes!

Broiled Beef Kabobs are a fun summer main dish seasoned in a snap with a tangy homemade marinade. "These kabobs are so simple to prepare," assures Margery Bryan of Royal City, Washington.

Apple-Nut Tossed Salad is a refreshing alternative to a plain lettuce salad. "We love the light dressing over crunchy apples, walnuts and lettuce sprinkled with blue cheese," remarks Maureen Reubelt of Gales Ferry, Connecticut.

Strawberry Lemon Parfaits make a cool, elegant dessert that's hardly any fuss to fix. The recipe for these pretty parfaits comes from Joy Beck of Cincinnati, Ohio.

Broiled Beef Kabobs

✓ Uses less fat, sugar or salt. Includes Nutritional Analysis and Diabetic Exchanges.

  1 tablespoon olive *or* vegetable oil
  1 tablespoon lemon juice
  1 tablespoon water
  2 teaspoons Dijon mustard
  1 teaspoon honey
1/2 teaspoon dried oregano
1/4 teaspoon pepper
  1 pound boneless top sirloin steak (1 inch thick), cut into 1-inch cubes
  2 small green *and/or* sweet red peppers, cut into 1-inch pieces
 12 large fresh mushrooms
Hot cooked rice

In a bowl, combine the first seven ingredients; mix well. Add beef, peppers and mushrooms; toss to coat. Thread meat and vegetables alternately on metal or soaked wooden skewers. Broil 3 in. from the heat, turning often, until meat reaches desired doneness and vegetables are tender, about 12-16 minutes. Serve over rice. **Yield:** 4 servings. **Nutritional Analysis:** One serving (calculated without rice) equals 231 calories, 122 mg sodium, 75 mg cholesterol, 8 gm carbohydrate, 28 gm protein, 10 gm fat. **Diabetic Exchanges:** 3-1/2 lean meat, 1-1/2 vegetable.

Apple-Nut Tossed Salad

  3 tablespoons olive *or* vegetable oil
  1 teaspoon Dijon mustard
3/4 teaspoon sugar
Salt and pepper to taste
1/2 cup chopped apple
  1 tablespoon chopped green onion
  3 cups torn Bibb lettuce
  1 to 2 tablespoons chopped walnuts
  1 to 2 tablespoons crumbled blue cheese

In a bowl, combine oil, mustard, sugar, salt and pepper. Add apple and onion; toss to coat. Add lettuce, walnuts and blue cheese; toss gently. Serve immediately. **Yield:** 4 servings.

Strawberry Lemon Parfaits

✓ Uses less fat, sugar or salt. Includes Nutritional Analysis and Diabetic Exchanges.

  1 pint fresh strawberries
  3 tablespoons sugar
  3 cartons (8 ounces *each*) lemon yogurt

In a food processor, combine strawberries and sugar. Process for 20-30 seconds or until berries are coarsely chopped. Divide half of the mixture into four parfait glasses. Top with yogurt and remaining berries. **Yield:** 4 servings. **Nutritional Analysis:** One serving (prepared with nonfat yogurt) equals 109 calories, 40 mg sodium, 1 mg cholesterol, 24 gm carbohydrate, 3 gm protein, trace fat. **Diabetic Exchanges:** 1 fruit, 1/2 skim milk.

> ### Berry Basics
> Buy plump strawberries with bright green caps and a nice red color. Store them in an uncovered colander or container in the refrigerator. Don't wash or hull the berries until you're ready to use them.

Good Morning, Sunshine!

SET A PRETTY TABLE and present your family with some tasty down-home cooking. It's guaranteed to make an ordinary day extra-special. Served beside a fresh fruit garnish, Calico Scrambled Eggs satisfy any hungry appetite. And fun-filled Sausage Breadsticks will appeal to kids of all ages. For a unique dessert, impress breakfast guests with easy Tropical Banana Compote...they'll certainly savor the old-fashioned flavor.

Calico Scrambled Eggs

When you're short on time and scrambling to get a meal on the table, this recipe is "eggs-actly" what you need. There's a short ingredient list, and cooking is kept to a minimum. Plus, with green pepper and tomato, it's colorful.

- 1/2 cup chopped green pepper
- 1/4 cup chopped onion
- 1 tablespoon butter *or* margarine
- 8 eggs
- 1/4 cup milk
- 1/8 to 1/4 teaspoon dill weed
- 1/8 to 1/4 teaspoon salt
- 1/8 to 1/4 teaspoon pepper
- 1/2 cup chopped fresh tomato

In a 12-in. nonstick skillet, saute green pepper and onion in butter until tender. Remove and set aside. In a medium bowl, beat eggs with milk, dill, salt and pepper. Pour into the skillet; cook and stir gently over medium heat until eggs are nearly set. Add pepper mixture and tomato; cook and stir until heated through and the eggs are completely set. **Yield:** 4 servings.

Sausage Breadsticks

Bring out the kid in everyone by preparing pigs-in-a-blanket with sausage links and refrigerated breadsticks. This fun and festive finger food is a unique addition to a breakfast buffet. Or make a heaping plateful for a snack.

- 1 tube (11 ounces) refrigerated breadstick dough
- 8 smoked sausage links *or* hot dogs

Separate the dough into eight strips; unroll and wrap one strip around each sausage. Place on an ungreased baking sheet. Bake at 350° for 15-17 minutes or until golden brown. Serve warm. **Yield:** 4 servings. **Editor's Note:** You may use refrigerated crescent rolls in place of the breadsticks. Just roll up a sausage in each triangle and follow the package directions for baking temperature and time.

Tropical Banana Compote

Don't limit your use of bananas to the cereal bowl. Instead, send your family's taste buds on a "trip" to the tropics with this special speedy dessert. Bananas are available in every season...so this is bound to become a favorite all year-round.

   3 medium firm bananas
1/4 cup orange juice
   2 tablespoons butter *or* margarine
   3 tablespoons brown sugar

   2 tablespoons flaked coconut, toasted
Maraschino cherries *or* strawberries, optional

Cut bananas in half lengthwise, then cut crosswise into quarters. Arrange in a greased 11-in. x 7-in. x 2-in. baking dish. In a saucepan, combine orange juice, butter and brown sugar; cook and stir until sugar is dissolved and butter is melted. Pour over the bananas. Bake, uncovered, at 350° for 10-12 minutes. Spoon into individual serving dishes; sprinkle with coconut. Garnish with cherries or strawberries if desired. **Yield:** 4 servings.

Thanksgiving Feast

THIS TIMELESS traditional fare means you don't have to wait for a holiday to bring a festive touch to your table. Turkey with Cranberry Sauce features a succulent tangy topping for the tender meat. Looking for some speedy side dishes? Walnut Stuffing Balls are fresh from the oven in no time…while Carrot Saute goes from stove to table in minutes. The meal is complete served with sweet apple cider.

Turkey with Cranberry Sauce

You'll hear rave reviews when fantastic fowl stars as the flavorful fare on your weekday menu. Cooking the turkey in butter and oil locks in the succulent juices. And what's turkey without cranberries? This tangy sauce is served right on top!

> 2 **turkey breast tenderloins (1 to 1-1/2 pounds)**
> 1/2 **teaspoon poultry seasoning**
> 1 **tablespoon vegetable oil**
> 1 **tablespoon butter** *or* **margarine**
> 1 **cup whole-berry cranberry sauce**
> 3 **tablespoons apple jelly**
> 3/4 **teaspoon Dijon mustard**
> 1/4 **teaspoon ground allspice**

Cut tenderloins crosswise in half. Slice each half lengthwise in half, but do not cut all the way through. Open and flatten each piece. Sprinkle both sides with poultry seasoning. In a large skillet over medium-high heat, cook turkey in oil and butter for 3-4 minutes on each side. Reduce heat to medium-low; cover and cook for 12-15 minutes or until juices run clear. Remove turkey to a platter and keep warm. Add cranberry sauce, jelly, mustard and allspice to skillet; simmer for 2-3 minutes. Spoon over turkey. **Yield:** 4 servings.

Walnut Stuffing Balls

Don't forget the stuffing even though you're not preparing a whole turkey. Your family will be happy to see these perfectly portioned stuffing balls on their plates …and you will be delighted to know they take just minutes to put together and bake.

> 1/3 **cup** *each* **chopped celery, green pepper and onion**
> 1/3 **cup chopped walnuts**
> 2 **tablespoons butter** *or* **margarine**
> 1 **egg**
> 3 **cups herb-seasoned stuffing croutons**
> 1/2 **cup chicken broth**
> 1/4 **teaspoon salt**
> 1/4 **teaspoon pepper**

In a saucepan, saute celery, green pepper, onion and walnuts in butter until vegetables are tender;

cool slightly. In a bowl, beat the egg. Add croutons, broth, salt, pepper and vegetable mixture; mix well. Shape into 12 balls, 1/4 cup each; place on a greased baking sheet. Bake at 375° for 20 minutes or until heated through. **Yield:** 4 servings.

Carrot Saute

Every cook knows delicious carrots don't need to be disguised with lots of seasonings. Simply saute them, *then sprinkle with some fresh chives and garlic salt.*

> 3 cups sliced *or* baby carrots
> 1 tablespoon finely chopped onion
> 1 to 2 tablespoons butter *or* margarine
> 2 tablespoons chopped chives
> 1/8 teaspoon garlic salt

In a medium skillet, saute carrots and onion in butter for 4 minutes; reduce heat. Cover and cook for 8-10 minutes or until carrots are tender. Toss with chives and garlic salt. **Yield:** 4 servings.

Hot Dogs with Fixin's Are A Grand-Slam Hit

GATHERING before the big game, hosting a family picnic or throwing a birthday bash? This fun-filled fuss-free meal is sure to be a hit.

You'll score points with kids of all ages when you set out this summertime spread. Everyone is sure to come running when dressed-up hot dogs, an appealing salad and a lip-smackin' pie are part of the lineup. Plates will be cleared off as quick as you put the popular foods together!

Chili Dogs made with a super zesty sauce are a super summer main dish, says Linda Rainey from her Monahans, Texas home. "I got the recipe for the hearty sauce more than 20 years ago from an aunt who lived in Chicago," Linda comments. "We love it at home or on a picnic."

Vicky Rader of Mullinville, Kansas also shares an all-in-the-family favorite. "My aunt traveled the world over and brought the recipe for Tomato Avocado Salad back with her from the Middle East," relates Vicky. "It's so colorful and simple to make."

Lemonade Pie is a refreshing dessert perfect for a summer meal. From Wilma Rusk of Bringhurst, Indiana, this cool, creamy sweet/tart pie hits the spot on a hot day…and you don't have to heat the oven to make it! With its ease of preparation, this recipe is a great way to get kids helping in the kitchen.

Tomato Avocado Salad

2 ripe avocados, peeled and sliced
2 large tomatoes, cut into wedges
1 medium onion, cut into wedges
1 cup Italian salad dressing
Lettuce leaves, optional

In a bowl, combine the avocados, tomatoes and onion; add dressing and stir to coat. Chill for 20-30 minutes. Serve over lettuce if desired. **Yield:** 6-8 servings.

Lemonade Pie

1 can (14 ounces) sweetened condensed milk
3/4 cup lemonade concentrate
2 to 3 drops yellow food coloring, optional
1 carton (8 ounces) frozen whipped topping, thawed
1 graham cracker crust (8 inches)
Lemon slices and fresh mint, optional

In a large bowl, combine milk, lemonade and food coloring if desired. Fold in the whipped topping; spoon into crust. Chill until serving. If desired, garnish with lemon slices and mint. **Yield:** 6-8 servings.

Chili Dogs

1 pound ground beef
1 garlic clove, minced
1 cup tomato juice
1 can (6 ounces) tomato paste
2 tablespoons chili powder
1 teaspoon hot pepper sauce
1 teaspoon salt
1/4 teaspoon pepper
8 hot dogs, cooked
8 hot dog buns
Chopped onion and shredded cheddar cheese, optional

In a large skillet, brown beef and garlic; drain. Stir in next six ingredients. Simmer, uncovered, for 20 minutes. Serve over hot dogs on buns. Top with onion and cheese if desired. **Yield:** 8 servings.

Avocado Advice

When purchasing avocados, think about how you'll be using them. If you'll be slicing and chopping them, look for ripe avocados that are slightly firm. If you'll be mashing the pulp, select very ripe avocados that feel soft. Avoid bruised fruit.

Refrigerate avocados and use within a few days after they're first purchased. To speed the ripening process of very firm avocados, place them in a brown paper bag.

To seed an avocado, cut lengthwise through the fruit around the seed. Separate the halves by twisting them in opposite directions; remove seed. Peel each half and slice. Or scoop out the pulp.

Yummy Yuletide Treats

WHEN THE FAMILY gathers for an old-fashioned tree-trimming party, serve up newfound favorites like saucy Stroganoff Meatballs. No one will be able to eat just one! With four simply satisfying ingredients, Holiday Pasta Toss will become a much-requested recipe year-round. And for dessert, why not dip into chocolaty Peppermint Fondue with an assortment of store-bought or homemade cookies?

Stroganoff Meatballs

For even quicker preparation, make these meatballs ahead of time and freeze. Then thaw, combine with the creamy sauce and warm in a chafing dish.

    1 egg
  1/2 cup dry bread crumbs
  1/4 cup milk
    1 tablespoon dried minced onion
    1 tablespoon dried parsley flakes
  1/4 teaspoon garlic salt
  1/4 teaspoon pepper
    1 pound ground beef
SAUCE:
    1 can (10-3/4 ounces) condensed cream of
      mushroom soup, undiluted
  1/2 cup sour cream
    2 tablespoons chili sauce
  1/4 teaspoon dried oregano
  1/4 teaspoon pepper
  1/8 teaspoon garlic salt

In a large bowl, beat the egg; add the next six ingredients. Add the beef and mix well. Shape into 1-in. balls; place on ungreased baking sheets. Bake, uncovered, at 450° for 12-15 minutes or until no longer pink. Drain on paper towels; place meatballs in a serving dish and keep warm. Combine all of the sauce ingredients in a medium saucepan; cook and stir until well blended and heated through. Spoon over meatballs. **Yield:** 4 servings.

Perfect Pasta

Your pasta will turn out wonderfully every time if you cook it, uncovered, at a fast boil. Also, be sure to stir it frequently as it cooks.

Holiday Pasta Toss

This recipe uses frozen spinach, so it's always in season. Plus, you can add other produce if you'd like. It's great month after month.

    2 cups uncooked spiral pasta
  1/4 to 1/3 cup Italian salad dressing
    1 package (10 ounces) frozen chopped
      spinach, thawed and drained
    1 teaspoon poppy seeds, optional

In a large saucepan, cook the pasta according to package directions; drain. In the same pan, heat dressing and spinach over medium heat. Return pasta to pan and toss to coat. Sprinkle with poppy seeds if desired. **Yield:** 4 servings.

———— ∽∽ ————

Peppermint Fondue

When your festive meal is over, continue the celebration by gathering around the fondue pot. Everyone will *enjoy dipping cookies into this chocolaty concoction...but they'll have an even better time gobbling up the fabulous results!*

> **12 ounces chocolate-covered peppermint patties, coarsely chopped**
> **1/4 cup milk**
> **Butter cookies**

In a medium saucepan over low heat, melt peppermint patties with milk, stirring frequently. Serve warm, using the cookies for dipping. **Yield:** 1 cup sauce.

Valentine's Day Delights

SHOW YOUR LOVED ONES you care by preparing a festive meal that comes straight from the heart! Your family will be pleasantly surprised when they see and taste Cheesy Chicken Pizza. It's packed with delicious toppings, like cheese, onions and peppers.

Italian Salad—featuring homemade dressing and your favorite greens—adds plenty of "zip" to the meal. For a special dessert, why not whip up chocolaty Mint Truffles? They're fancy yet fast, and they'll be gobbled up before you know it.

Cheesy Chicken Pizza

Why pop a frozen pizza in the oven when you can serve your family generous slices of this fast and flavorful pizza pie? Chicken provides a unique change of pace from the usual beef or pepperoni...and it pairs nicely with the onion, peppers and cheese.

- **1 tube (10 ounces) refrigerated pizza crust dough**
- **1 can (8 ounces) pizza sauce**
- **1/2 cup diced cooked chicken**
- **1 small onion, sliced**
- **1/4 cup sliced green pepper**
- **1/4 cup sliced sweet red pepper**
- **1 cup (4 ounces) shredded cheddar cheese**
- **1 cup (4 ounces) shredded mozzarella cheese**

Unroll pizza crust onto a greased baking sheet; form into a heart shape or a 12-in. circle. Spread with pizza sauce. Top with the chicken, onion and peppers. Sprinkle with cheeses. Bake on lowest rack at 425° for 16-20 minutes or until crust is dark golden brown. **Yield:** 4 servings.

Italian Salad

Salad's never been speedier than this! Gather up a few greens and vegetables, then make your own dressing by mixing together a mere five ingredients you most likely have right on hand.

- **1/4 cup olive *or* vegetable oil**

- **1/4 cup cider *or* red wine vinegar**
- **1/2 teaspoon Italian seasoning**
- **1/4 teaspoon salt**
- **1/4 teaspoon coarsely ground black pepper**
- **Romaine *or* other lettuce**
- **Tomatoes, mushrooms, cucumber, olives *and/or* other vegetables of choice**
- **Shredded Parmesan cheese, optional**

In a jar with tight-fitting lid, combine the oil, vinegar, Italian seasoning, salt and pepper; shake well. In a large bowl, combine lettuce and vegetables. Add the dressing and Parmesan cheese if desired; toss to coat. **Yield:** 1/2 cup dressing.

Mint Truffles

These chocolaty candies have such an appealing look and sweet flavor, it's hard to believe they take only minutes to prepare. They're the perfect thing to serve for both everyday treats and special-occasion desserts.

1 cup (6 ounces) milk chocolate chips
3/4 cup whipped topping
1/4 teaspoon peppermint extract
2 tablespoons baking cocoa

In a small saucepan, melt chocolate chips over low heat. Place in a mixing bowl and allow to cool to lukewarm, about 7 minutes. Beat in whipped topping and extract. Place in freezer for 15 minutes or until firm enough to form into balls. Shape into 1-in. balls. Roll in cocoa. Store in a covered container in the refrigerator. **Yield:** about 1 dozen.

Salad in a Snap

Speed up salad making by washing, drying and cutting all ingredients as soon as you have them in the kitchen. Then store in a plastic bag. At mealtime, just pull out the bag and make the salad.

Rise and Shine with Bright Breakfast

WHEN YOUR ALARM CLOCK rings, the hustle and bustle of your day begins. So, why not get your day off to a good start with a hearty, wholesome breakfast?

Ready to serve in just 30 minutes, the delightful breakfast or brunch menu here makes a mouth-watering morning meal.

Oven Denver Omelet is suggested by Ellen Bower of Taneytown, Maryland. "I like omelets but don't always have time to stand by the stove. That's why I favor this oven-baked variety that I can quickly pop into the oven at a moment's notice," she notes. "My family frequently requests this for Sunday brunch. They always empty the dish." Chopped fresh mushrooms would be a nice addition to this enticing omelet.

Raspberry Lemon Muffins are a tart treat to eat along with a meal or as a snack. Says Georgia Carruthers of Livonia, Michigan, "I collect bread and muffin recipes, and this is one of my favorites." You can easily substitute fresh or frozen blueberries for the raspberries if you prefer. Plus, these muffins freeze well, so they're easy to have on hand.

Golden Smoothies take no more effort to whip up than orange juice from concentrate, relates Nancy Schmidt of Delhi, California. "A tall glass of this rich, smooth eye-opener makes any morning special," she adds.

―――――――― ∞∽∞ ――――――――

Oven Denver Omelet

      8 eggs
  1/2 cup half-and-half cream
      1 cup (4 ounces) shredded cheddar cheese
      1 cup finely chopped fully cooked ham
  1/4 cup finely chopped green pepper
  1/4 cup finely chopped onion

In a bowl, beat eggs and cream until light and fluffy. Stir in the cheese, ham, green pepper and onion. Pour into a greased 9-in. square baking dish. Bake at 400° for 25 minutes or until golden brown. **Yield:** 4-6 servings.

―――――――― ∞∽∞ ――――――――

Raspberry Lemon Muffins

      2 cups all-purpose flour
  1/2 cup sugar
      1 teaspoon baking powder
      1 teaspoon baking soda
  1/2 teaspoon salt
      2 eggs, lightly beaten
      1 cup (8 ounces) lemon yogurt
  1/4 cup butter *or* margarine, melted and cooled
      1 teaspoon grated lemon peel
      1 teaspoon vanilla extract
  1-1/2 cups fresh *or* frozen raspberries

In a bowl, combine flour, sugar, baking powder, baking soda and salt. Combine eggs, yogurt, butter, lemon peel and vanilla; mix well. Stir into dry ingredients just until moistened. Fold in raspberries. Fill greased or paper-lined muffin cups three-fourths full. Bake at 400° for 18-20 minutes or until muffins test done. **Yield:** 1 dozen.

―――――――― ∞∽∞ ――――――――

Golden Smoothies

☑ Uses less fat, sugar or salt. Includes Nutritional Analysis and Diabetic Exchanges.

  1-1/2 cups orange juice
      1 carton (8 ounces) peach yogurt
      1 can (5-1/2 ounces) apricot nectar
      1 teaspoon honey
  Orange slices and maraschino cherries, optional

Place the first four ingredients in a blender; cover and process until smooth. Pour into glasses; garnish with oranges and cherries if desired. **Yield:** 3 cups. **Nutritional Analysis:** One 3/4-cup serving (prepared with fat-free yogurt; calculated without fruit garnish) equals 128 calories, 37 mg sodium, 2 mg cholesterol, 29 gm carbohydrate, 3 gm protein, trace fat. **Diabetic Exchanges:** 1 skim milk, 1 fruit.

Egg Basics

At the store, only purchase eggs stored in the refrigerator case and put them into your refrigerator as soon as you get home. To help prevent eggs from picking up odors and flavors from other foods in the refrigerator, it's best to store eggs in their original carton.

Springtime Sensations

CELEBRATE SPRING with family and friends by serving this formal no-fuss dinner. Mustard Pork Medallions pop in the oven for a main dish in a flash. Dilly Asparagus, delicately topped with an easy-to-prepare cream cheese sauce, and your favorite dinner rolls make outstanding additions. For a fantastic finale, Rhubarb Sundaes are simply delicious.

—————————— ✤ ——————————

Mustard Pork Medallions

Your famished family will be thrilled when you call them to the dinner table with the irresistible aroma of these tasty pork medallions. Brushing the pork with mustard and coating it with seasoned dry bread crumbs before you bake it make the meat tender and juicy every time.

☑ Uses less fat, sugar or salt. Includes Nutritional Analysis and Diabetic Exchanges.

    1/2 cup seasoned dry bread crumbs
    1/2 teaspoon dried thyme
    1/4 teaspoon garlic salt
    1/4 teaspoon onion powder
  1-1/4 pounds pork tenderloin
    1/4 cup Dijon mustard
      1 tablespoon butter *or* margarine, melted

In a shallow bowl, combine the crumbs, thyme, garlic salt and onion powder; set aside. Cut tenderloin crosswise into 12 pieces and pound each piece to 1/4-in. thickness. Combine mustard and butter; brush on each side of pork, then coat with reserved crumb mixture. Place in a greased shallow baking pan. Bake, uncovered, at 425° for 10 minutes; turn and bake about 5 minutes more or until no longer pink. **Yield:** 4 servings. **Nutritional Analysis:** One serving (prepared with margarine) equals 254 calories, 855 mg sodium, 53 mg cholesterol, 15 gm carbohydrate, 25 gm protein, 11 gm fat. **Diabetic Exchanges:** 3 lean meat, 1 starch, 1/2 fat.

—————————— ✤ ——————————

Dilly Asparagus

A sure sign of spring is a fresh crop of young asparagus. And this recipe superbly ushers in this wonderful season. A delicate cheese sauce nicely complements tender stalks without being overwhelming.

      1 cup water
    1/4 teaspoon salt
      1 pound fresh asparagus, trimmed
      1 package (3 ounces) cream cheese
    1/2 cup milk
    1/4 teaspoon dill weed
    1/8 teaspoon garlic salt
    1/8 teaspoon pepper

In a large skillet, bring water and salt to a boil; add the asparagus. Cover and cook over medium heat until crisp-tender, about 6-8 minutes; drain.

Transfer to a serving platter and keep warm. In the same skillet over low heat, stir cream cheese and milk until smooth. Stir in dill, garlic salt and pepper. Pour over asparagus. **Yield:** 4 servings.

———————⌒∽∾⌒———————

Rhubarb Sundaes

After one taste, your family will agree rhubarb never tasted so good! The sweet sauce will disappear so fast when you serve it over ice cream that you might want to keep some on hand to serve over pancakes, waffles...even French toast.

> 2 **cups chopped fresh** *or* **frozen rhubarb**
> 1/4 **cup water**
> 1/3 **cup sugar**
> 1/4 **teaspoon ground cinnamon**
> 1/2 **teaspoon honey**
> **Vanilla ice cream**
> **Chopped walnuts, optional**

In a saucepan, bring rhubarb, water, sugar and cinnamon to a boil. Reduce heat; simmer, uncovered, for 8-10 minutes or until rhubarb is tender and the sauce has reached desired consistency. Remove from the heat; stir in honey. Serve warm over ice cream. Sprinkle with nuts if desired. **Yield:** 4 servings (1 cup sauce).

Hearty Sandwiches Are Sure to Please!

IF HOBBIES and other activities limit the amount of time you spend in the kitchen, this classic combination is sure to catch your interest.

The satisfying sandwich and salad and old-fashioned ice cream dessert can be on the dinner table in about 30 minutes!

"Honey-Mustard Chicken Sandwiches are homemade 'fast food' that's more delicious than the kind you go out to pick up," assures Christina Levrant of Bensalem, Pennsylvania. The special sauce has just the right amount of sweetness and tang.

Black 'n' White Bean Salad is a cool, hearty side dish Kay Ogden created after tasting a similar one in a restaurant. "It goes together in no time and complements most entrees," she reports from her Grants Pass, Oregon home.

Quick Banana Splits are a simple but special way to serve ice cream. The recipe comes from Doreen Stein of Ignace, Ontario.

Honey-Mustard Chicken Sandwiches

☑ Uses less fat, sugar or salt. Includes Nutritional Analysis and Diabetic Exchanges.

    1/4 cup Dijon mustard
    2 tablespoons honey
    1 teaspoon dried oregano
    1 teaspoon water
    1/4 teaspoon garlic powder
    1/8 to 1/4 teaspoon cayenne pepper
    4 boneless skinless chicken breast halves
      (1 pound)
    4 sandwich buns, split
    8 thin tomato slices
    1 cup shredded lettuce

In a bowl, combine the first six ingredients. Broil chicken 4 in. from the heat for 3 minutes on each side. Brush with mustard sauce. Broil 4-6 minutes longer or until juices run clear, basting and turning several times. Serve on buns with tomato and lettuce. **Yield:** 4 servings. **Nutritional Analysis:** One serving (calculated without bun) equals 185 calories, 438 mg sodium, 63 mg cholesterol, 13 gm carbohydrate, 24 gm protein, 4 gm fat. **Diabetic Exchanges:** 3 very lean meat, 1 starch.

Black 'n' White Bean Salad

☑ Uses less fat, sugar or salt. Includes Nutritional Analysis and Diabetic Exchanges.

    1 can (15 ounces) black beans, rinsed and
      drained
    1 can (15 ounces) white kidney beans,
      rinsed and drained
    1/2 cup chopped cucumber
    1/2 cup chopped sweet red pepper
    1/4 cup chopped onion
    1/4 cup minced fresh cilantro or parsley
    1/3 cup cider or red wine vinegar
    1/4 cup olive or vegetable oil
    1/2 teaspoon salt, optional
    1/4 teaspoon garlic powder
    1/8 teaspoon pepper
Lettuce leaves, optional

In a large bowl, combine the first six ingredients. In a small bowl, whisk vinegar, oil and seasonings. Pour over bean mixture and toss to coat. Cover and refrigerate until serving. Using a slotted spoon, serve over lettuce if desired. **Yield:** 4-6 servings. **Nutritional Analysis:** One 1/2-cup serving (prepared without salt) equals 187 calories, 219 mg sodium, 0 cholesterol, 26 gm carbohydrate, 9 gm protein, 5 gm fat. **Diabetic Exchanges:** 1-1/2 starch, 1 vegetable, 1 fat.

Quick Banana Splits

    2 medium bananas
    1 pint vanilla ice cream
Chocolate syrup or ice cream topping
Chopped nuts
Maraschino cherries

Slice bananas into four dessert dishes. Top each with 1/2 cup of ice cream. Drizzle with chocolate syrup. Sprinkle with nuts; top with cherries. **Yield:** 4 servings.

Honey of a Hint

To easily remove honey from a measuring spoon, first coat the spoon with nonstick cooking spray.

Hurry-Up Holiday Meal

THE HOLIDAYS can be a hectic time, leaving little time to prepare an elaborate meal. So why not present yourself and your hungry clan with this festive *and* fast meal highlighting Pork with Mushroom Sauce that looks like it took hours to prepare?

Deliciously cheesy Topped Taters are made extra-easy by using leftover spuds. With their cool minty flavor, Peppermint Parfaits are the perfect ending to your favorite meals…any time of year!

Pork with Mushroom Sauce

Treat your family to a festive meal of pork tenderloin without spending hours in the kitchen. It's easy enough to prepare for weekday dinners and impressive enough to serve on special occasions.

> 1 pork tenderloin (about 1 pound)
> 3 tablespoons butter *or* margarine
> 1/2 teaspoon dried thyme
> 1/2 teaspoon salt
> 1/4 teaspoon pepper
> 1 cup sliced fresh mushrooms
> 1 small onion, sliced
> 2/3 cup milk
> 1 tablespoon Dijon mustard
> 1-1/2 teaspoons cornstarch

Cut tenderloin crosswise into fourths. Slice each piece in half but do not cut all the way through; open and flatten each piece. Melt butter in a large skillet; add pork. Combine thyme, salt and pepper; sprinkle half over the meat. Cook 3-4 minutes per side. Add mushrooms and onion. Cook and stir until vegetables are almost tender and pork is no longer pink. Remove meat to a platter and keep warm. Combine milk, mustard, cornstarch and the remaining thyme mixture; stir into the vegetables. Bring to a boil; cook and stir for 2 minutes. Spoon over pork and serve immediately. **Yield:** 4 servings.

Topped Taters

Leftover mashed potatoes don't have to be plain and boring. Simply stir in sour cream and onions and top with cheese for a creative new way to serve taters.

> 3 cups leftover mashed potatoes
> 3/4 cup sour cream, *divided*
> 3 tablespoons sliced green onions with tops, *divided*
> 1/4 to 1/2 teaspoon garlic salt
> 1/2 cup shredded cheddar cheese

Combine the potatoes, 1/4 cup of sour cream, 1 tablespoon green onions and the garlic salt; mix well. Spoon into a greased 1-qt. baking dish. Cover and bake at 350° for 20 minutes. Uncover; spread with the remaining sour cream. Sprinkle with the cheese and remaining onions. Return to the oven for 5 minutes or until the cheese is melted. **Yield:** 4 servings.

Peppermint Parfaits

Nothing is as pleasing to your palate after a satisfying meal like mint. These easy-to-prepare peppermint parfaits are the perfect way to end any meal.

   24 large marshmallows
  1/2 cup milk
    1 teaspoon vanilla extract
Pinch salt
  1/4 teaspoon peppermint extract
    5 to 8 drops red food coloring
    2 cups whipped topping
Crushed chocolate wafers

In a saucepan over low heat, melt marshmallows with milk. Remove from the heat; stir in vanilla, salt, extract and food coloring. Chill for 10 minutes; fold in whipped topping. Spoon into individual dishes. Chill until serving. Garnish with chocolate wafers. **Yield:** 4 servings.

Splendid Spuds

To make mashed potatoes hold their shape when topping a casserole or shepherd's pie, thicken them by beating in an egg yolk or two instead of milk.

Instead of adding whole milk to mashed potatoes, reserve some of the water used to boil the potatoes and mix in powdered milk. This retains the nutrients (and potato flavor) in the water...and it's economical, too.

Finger-Licking-Good Fixin's

WITH THE WARM autumn sun shining on a cool, crisp day, round up relatives and friends for a spur-of-the-moment outing featuring all-time favorite foods. Because it's skillet-fried, traditional Picnic Chicken couldn't be easier to assemble. You can use the last of your garden's bounty in Citrus Tossed Salad. And don't forget to pass a basket brimming with slightly sweet Cinnamon Biscuits.

Picnic Chicken

Whether you're gathering for a picnic in the park or a get-together in the backyard, this pan-fried chicken is the perfect entree. It's moist inside, crispy outside...and goes from skillet to table in no time!

- **4 boneless skinless chicken breast halves**
- **1 cup dry bread crumbs**
- **1/2 teaspoon dried parsley flakes**
- **1/2 teaspoon garlic salt**
- **1/4 teaspoon pepper**
- **1/4 teaspoon paprika**
- **1/8 teaspoon dried thyme**
- **1 egg, lightly beaten**
- **1 tablespoon vegetable oil**
- **1 tablespoon butter *or* margarine**

Pound chicken to 1/4-in. thickness. In a shallow bowl, combine bread crumbs and seasonings. Dip chicken in egg, then in the crumb mixture. In a skillet, brown the chicken in oil and butter over medium heat for 3-5 minutes on each side or until juices run clear. **Yield:** 4 servings.

Citrus Tossed Salad

Reach for this recipe when you want a nicely tangy change of pace from ordinary salads. Everyday ingredients come together in a delightful dressing that enhances the greens, vegetables, oranges and walnuts.

- **3 tablespoons olive *or* vegetable oil**
- **2 teaspoons orange juice**
- **1/2 teaspoon sugar**
- **1/2 teaspoon honey**
- **1/2 teaspoon Dijon mustard**
- **1/2 teaspoon lemon juice**
- **1/8 teaspoon grated orange peel**
- **1/8 teaspoon salt**
- **1/8 teaspoon pepper**
- **Dash onion powder**
- **6 cups torn romaine *or* other greens**
- **1/2 cup *each* sliced fresh mushrooms, sweet red pepper and red onion**
- **1/2 cup mandarin oranges**
- **1/4 cup chopped walnuts, optional**

In a jar with a tight-fitting lid, combine the first 10 ingredients and shake well. In a large salad bowl, combine lettuce, vegetables, oranges and walnuts

if desired. Just before serving, add dressing and toss to coat. **Yield:** 4 servings.

Cinnamon Biscuits

These oven-fresh biscuits will disappear from your table as quickly as it took to prepare them! But you can easily whip up another batch. Serve them with fried chicken, at breakfast or as a savory snack.

2 cups all-purpose flour
1 tablespoon baking powder
2 teaspoons sugar
1/2 teaspoon salt
1/4 teaspoon ground cinnamon
1/4 cup cold butter *or* margarine
1 cup milk
Melted butter *or* margarine
Cinnamon-sugar

In a bowl, combine dry ingredients; cut in butter until crumbly. Stir in milk just until moistened. Drop by 1/4 cupfuls onto a greased baking sheet. Brush with melted butter and sprinkle with cinnamon-sugar. Bake at 450° for 10-12 minutes or until lightly browned. Serve warm. **Yield:** about 1 dozen.

Family-Pleasing Feast Cooks Up in a Flash

WITH PRESENTS to wrap, cards to send and the many other holiday activities filling up your days, time is short to prepare your family a satisfying supper. This family-pleasing spread is the perfect solution. You can sit down to a relaxing dinner in under half an hour.

Microwave Parmesan Chicken comes from Ruth Andrewson of Leavenworth, Washington. She says, "The golden coating over moist chicken makes people think you fussed."

Festive Green Beans can't be beat for a vegetable dish that sports the colors of the season and gets people coming back for seconds, assures Frances Janssen of Canyon Lake, Texas, who notes that this is a side dish her whole family enjoys. Made with Mexican-style stewed tomatoes or salsa, it has zip.

Cookies in a Jiffy are from Clara Hielkema of Wyoming, Michigan. She reports you'll be amazed and delighted at how quickly you can whip up a batch of homemade cookies.

Microwave Parmesan Chicken

1/4 cup butter *or* margarine
3/4 cup crushed butter-flavored crackers
1/2 cup grated Parmesan cheese
1 tablespoon dried minced onion
1 tablespoon dried parsley flakes
1/2 teaspoon garlic powder
1/8 teaspoon pepper
1 broiler-fryer chicken (2-1/2 to 3 pounds), cut up

Melt butter in a 13-in. x 9-in. x 2-in. microwave-safe baking dish. In a shallow bowl, combine the next six ingredients. Dredge chicken in butter, then in crumb mixture. Place chicken in the baking dish, with skin side up and thick edges toward the outside. Sprinkle with remaining crumb mixture. Microwave on high for 20-25 minutes or until juices run clear and chicken is no longer pink, rotating dish occasionally. **Yield:** 4-6 servings. **Editor's Note:** This recipe was tested using a 700-watt microwave.

Festive Green Beans

✓ Uses less fat, sugar or salt. Includes Nutritional Analysis and Diabetic Exchanges.

1 pound fresh green beans *or* 1 can (16 ounces) green beans, drained
1/2 cup water
1/2 teaspoon salt, optional
1/4 teaspoon pepper
1/2 teaspoon garlic powder
3/4 cup Mexican stewed tomatoes *or* chunky salsa

Cut beans into 2-in. pieces; place in a saucepan. Add water and salt if desired; bring to a boil. Reduce heat and simmer for 15 minutes or until tender; drain. Add pepper, garlic powder and tomatoes; heat through. **Yield:** 6 servings. **Nutritional Analysis:** One 1/2-cup serving (prepared with fresh beans and salsa and without salt) equals 35 calories, 225 mg sodium, 0 cholesterol, 8 gm carbohydrate, 1 gm protein, trace fat. **Diabetic Exchange:** 1-1/2 vegetable.

Cookies in a Jiffy

1 package (9 ounces) yellow cake mix
2/3 cup quick-cooking oats
1/2 cup butter *or* margarine, melted
1 egg
1/2 cup red and green Holiday M&M's *or* butterscotch chips

In a mixing bowl, beat the first four ingredients. Stir in the M&M's or chips. Drop by tablespoonfuls 2 in. apart onto ungreased baking sheets. Bake at 375° for 10-12 minutes or until lightly browned. Remove to wire racks to cool. **Yield:** 2 dozen.

Extraordinary Beans

If you want to put some zip into an ordinary can of green beans, try adding a few shakes of seasoning salt and a couple drops of liquid smoke.

Rainy Day Dinner

IF APRIL SHOWERS won't go away and you're stuck inside the house all day, treat your restless family to this one-of-a-kind menu that you can take from start to finish at a moment's notice. Folks will surely fall for flaky Oven-Fried Fish…hook, line and sinker! Lemon Rice adds a subtle citrus taste to the table, and creative Raspberry Almond Rounds dress up refrigerated biscuit dough in a snap.

Oven-Fried Fish

When you're looking for a fast, flavorful meal, look no further than fish! Parmesan cheese and special seasonings add a bit of Italian flair to these fillets. Not only is this recipe low in fat, it's delicious as well. So it's sure to please everyone in the family.

☑ Uses less fat, sugar or salt. Includes Nutritional Analysis and Diabetic Exchanges.

1-1/2 **pounds frozen cod** *or* **haddock fillets, thawed**
   2 **tablespoons butter** *or* **margarine, melted**
 1/2 **cup crushed wheat crackers** *or* **seasoned dry bread crumbs**
   2 **tablespoons grated Parmesan cheese**
   1 **tablespoon dried parsley flakes**
 1/2 **teaspoon Italian seasoning**

Cut fish into serving-size pieces; place in a greased 13-in. x 9-in. x 2-in. baking dish. Brush with butter. Combine the remaining ingredients; sprinkle over fish. Bake, uncovered, at 425° for 10-15 minutes or until the fish flakes easily with a fork. **Yield:** 4 servings. **Nutritional Analysis:** One serving (prepared with margarine and bread crumbs) equals 261 calories, 753 mg sodium, 78 mg cholesterol, 15 gm carbohydrate, 30 gm protein, 9 gm fat. **Diabetic Exchanges:** 4 very lean meat, 1 starch, 1 fat.

Lemon Rice

This easy recipe pleasantly proves you can dress up regular rice with a few simple additions. Best of all, it can simmer while you're preparing the rest of the meal. These delicately lemon-flavored grains go nicely with fish.

   1 **cup water**
   1 **cup chicken broth**
   2 **tablespoons lemon juice**
   2 **teaspoons butter** *or* **margarine**
   1 **cup uncooked long grain rice**
 1/4 **teaspoon dried basil**
 1/8 **to 1/4 teaspoon grated lemon peel**
 1/4 **teaspoon lemon-pepper seasoning**

In a medium saucepan, bring water, broth, lemon juice and butter to a boil. Stir in the rice, basil and lemon peel. Reduce heat; cover and simmer for 20 minutes. Let stand 5 minutes or until the water is

absorbed. Before serving, sprinkle with lemon pepper. **Yield:** 4 servings.

Raspberry Almond Rounds

Folks will find these nutty raspberry rounds so enticing you may not want to divulge that the "secret" to their success begins with refrigerated biscuit dough! These sweet treats bake up in a hurry, so they're great to serve when unexpected company drops in.

2 tablespoons butter *or* margarine, melted

1 tube (7-1/2 ounces) refrigerated buttermilk biscuits, separated into 10 biscuits
2 tablespoons sugar
1/4 cup raspberry preserves
2 tablespoons slivered almonds

Brush butter on both sides of biscuits. Place on a greased baking sheet or in a greased 9-in. round baking pan; sprinkle with sugar. Make an indentation in the center of each biscuit; fill with 1 teaspoon preserves. Sprinkle almonds on top. Bake at 425° for 9-11 minutes or until golden brown. **Yield:** 4-6 servings.

Spooktacular Menu

AUTUMN brings with it cool, crisp days, and there's no better way to take the chill out of your family's bones than to have them sit down to a steaming-hot bowl of Pronto Chili loaded with meat, vegetables …and flavor!

Cornmeal Cheddar Biscuits are a perfect complement to this hearty chili, and because no rolling or cutting is required, you can have fresh-from-the-oven goodness in no time. And while your family is busy "goblin" up those deliciously satisfying dishes, individual Peanut Butter Tarts can be chilling in the meantime.

Pronto Chili

Your busy schedule doesn't always allow you to simmer chili all day long on the stove. But you don't have to wait until the weekend to make some. This chili can be made in a flash and is easily doubled or tripled to satisfy any famished family.

> 1 **pound ground beef**
> 1 **medium onion, chopped**
> 1 **medium green pepper, chopped**
> 2 **to 3 teaspoons chili powder**
> 1 **teaspoon ground cumin**
> 1 **teaspoon salt**
> 1 **can (14-1/2 ounces) Mexican stewed tomatoes**
> 1 **can (15-3/4 ounces) chili beans in gravy**
> 1 **cup frozen corn**

Shredded cheddar cheese, optional

In a 2-qt. saucepan, cook beef, onion and green pepper until the meat is browned and the vegetables are tender. Drain. Add the next six ingredients; cover and simmer for 20 minutes. Sprinkle individual servings with cheese if desired. **Yield:** 6 servings.

Cornmeal Cheddar Biscuits

Unlike traditional biscuits, this cheesy cornmeal version lets you drop them from a spoon…so there's no mess and no fuss…and no precious time wasted! Serve them fresh-from-the-oven with chili or your favorite soup or stew.

> 1-1/2 **cups all-purpose flour**
> 1/2 **cup yellow cornmeal**
> 2 **teaspoons sugar**
> 1 **tablespoon baking powder**
> 1/4 **to 1/2 teaspoon salt**
> 1/2 **cup cold butter** *or* **margarine**
> 1/2 **cup shredded cheddar cheese**
> 1 **cup milk**

In a bowl, combine dry ingredients; cut in butter until crumbly. Stir in cheese and milk just until moistened. Drop by 1/4 cupfuls onto an ungreased baking sheet. Bake at 450° for 12-15 minutes or until light golden brown. Serve warm. **Yield:** 1 dozen.

Peanut Butter Tarts

These tiny tarts taste delicious and are a fun and easy way to round out a meal. Children especially like having their own "little pie" to help decorate. Make these goodies throughout the year with an assortment of favorite candies. These tarts will surely become a big part of your recipe collection because they're so convenient—they chill while you're enjoying the rest of your meal.

1 cup peanut butter chips
1 tablespoon vegetable oil
1 package (3.9 ounces) instant chocolate
   pudding mix
1-3/4 cups cold milk
   1 package (6 count) individual graham
      cracker tart shells
Whipped topping
Halloween candy, sprinkles *and/or* cake
   decorations

In the top of a double boiler over simmering water, melt chips with oil, stirring until smooth. Remove top pan from water and cool for 5 minutes. Meanwhile, in a bowl, whisk pudding mix and milk until thick. Fold in peanut butter mixture. Spoon into tart shells. Chill for 15 minutes. Top with a dollop of whipped topping and decorate as desired. **Yield:** 6 servings.

July Fourth Favorites

YOU'RE BOUND TO CREATE fireworks when you present these favorites at your Independence Day picnic, especially when hearty helpings of a Turkey Hero are the main feature. Summertime Pasta Salad gets a new twist with its combination of frozen vegetables and salad dressings. And for the finale, get in the spirit with a Red, White and Blue Dessert of angel food cake and berries.

Turkey Hero

Who says sandwiches have to be boring? Here, a special cream cheese and ranch dressing spread adds zest to the hearty turkey, cheese and vegetables. Get set to slice up second helpings!

- 1 package (3 ounces) cream cheese, softened
- 2 tablespoons ranch salad dressing
- 1 teaspoon poppy seeds
- Pinch garlic powder
- 1 loaf (1 pound) French bread, split lengthwise
- Shredded lettuce
- 3/4 pound thinly sliced cooked turkey
- 1/4 pound thinly sliced Swiss cheese
- 2 medium tomatoes, sliced

In a small mixing bowl, beat the first four ingredients until smooth. Spread on both cut surfaces of bread. Layer lettuce, turkey, cheese and tomatoes on bottom half of bread. Top with the other half. Cut into serving-size pieces. **Yield:** 6 servings.

Summertime Pasta Salad

Nothing says summer quite like a cool pasta salad with loads of vegetables! Best of all, this recipe calls for frozen vegetables, so it's perfect when you don't have time to slice and dice fresh produce.

- 2-1/2 cups uncooked spiral pasta
- 1 package (10 ounces) frozen mixed vegetables
- 2/3 cup ranch salad dressing
- 1/3 cup Italian salad dressing
- 1/2 teaspoon dill weed
- 1/2 teaspoon garlic salt
- 2 small tomatoes, diced

In a large kettle, cook pasta according to package directions. Place frozen vegetables in a strainer. Pour cooked pasta and water over vegetables to thaw; rinse and drain well. In a small bowl or jar with tight-fitting lid, combine salad dressings, dill and garlic salt until smooth. Place pasta mixture in a large bowl. Add tomatoes and dressing; stir gently to coat. **Yield:** 6 servings.

Red, White and Blue Dessert

Beat the summer heat with this light and refreshing dessert. No one will be able to resist sweet raspberries and blueberries atop moist angel food cake.

    1 cup fresh raspberries
    1 cup fresh blueberries
    1/4 cup sugar
    1/2 teaspoon almond extract
    6 slices angel food cake

Combine raspberries and blueberries in a bowl. Sprinkle with sugar and extract; toss gently. Place cake on dessert plates and top with berry mixture. **Yield:** 6 servings.

Be Kind to Your Cake

If the top of your angel food cake burns before the rest of the cake is done, use an oven thermometer to make sure your oven is not baking at a higher temperature than you set it. Also, place the pan on the lowest rack to allow sufficient air circulation over the top of the cake.

Fall Feast Will Harvest Compliments

TIRED of traditional uses for leftover Thanksgiving turkey? Turn it into this second-time around supper without spending a lot of time in the kitchen. Your family is sure to be thankful.

Turkey in Curry Sauce is a delicious fall entree with a hint of curry flavor and crunchy nuts. "You can whip up this main dish in just minutes using leftover turkey," reports Lucile Proctor of Panguitch, Utah.

Peas with Mushrooms, from Mary Dennis of Bryan, Ohio, is a savory side dish with a fresh taste, even though it calls for convenient frozen peas.

Rich Chocolate Mousse will get raves for its big chocolate taste. The recipe comes from Florence Palmer of Marshall, Illinois, who remarks, "I love to serve this impressive dessert because people think I went to a lot of trouble. Actually, it's easy to make."

Turkey in Curry Sauce

1/2 cup chopped onion
1/4 cup butter *or* margarine
1/4 cup all-purpose flour
1 can (14-1/2 ounces) chicken broth
1 cup half-and-half cream
2 to 3 teaspoons curry powder
2 cups diced cooked turkey
2 tablespoons chopped pimientos
Hot cooked rice
1/2 cup chopped peanuts

In a saucepan, saute onion in butter until tender. Add flour to form a smooth paste. Gradually stir in broth; bring to a boil. Boil for 1-2 minutes or until thickened. Reduce heat. Add half-and-half cream and curry; mix well. Add turkey; heat through. Stir in pimientos. Serve over rice; sprinkle with peanuts. **Yield:** 4 servings.

Peas with Mushrooms

☑ Uses less fat, sugar or salt. Includes Nutritional Analysis and Diabetic Exchanges.

1/2 pound fresh mushrooms, sliced
2 tablespoons sliced green onions

1 tablespoon butter *or* margarine
1/4 teaspoon dried marjoram
1/4 teaspoon salt, optional
1/8 teaspoon pepper
Dash ground nutmeg
1 package (10 ounces) frozen peas, cooked

In a skillet over medium heat, saute the mushrooms and onions in butter for 3-5 minutes. Add marjoram, salt if desired, pepper and nutmeg; mix well. Add peas and heat through. **Yield:** 4 servings. **Nutritional Analysis:** One serving (prepared with margarine and without added salt) equals 95 calories, 117 mg sodium, 0 cholesterol, 10 gm carbohydrate, 4 gm protein, 3 gm fat. **Diabetic Exchanges:** 1 vegetable, 1/2 starch, 1/2 fat.

Rich Chocolate Mousse

8 squares (1 ounce *each*) semisweet chocolate
3 tablespoons confectioners' sugar
3 tablespoons hot strong coffee
3 egg yolks
1 carton (8 ounces) frozen whipped topping, thawed, *divided*

In a double boiler over simmering water, melt chocolate. Remove top pan from heat; stir in sugar and coffee. Add one yolk at a time, stirring until smooth. Place top pan over boiling water; cook and stir for 3-4 minutes or until thick. Pour into bowl; chill 6-8 minutes. Fold in 3 cups whipped topping. Spoon into dishes. Top with remaining whipped topping. **Yield:** 4 servings.

Poultry Pointers

The next time you roast a whole turkey or turkey breast, set aside 2 cups diced, cooked meat for this meal. Let cool completely and place in an airtight container. To prevent the turkey from drying out, cover with a damp paper towel; refrigerate for 3 to 4 days. For longer storage, freeze up to 3 months.

Supper Signals Spring

WARM WEATHER has arrived, so serve up a garden-fresh goody like Sesame Asparagus. Your family will love its slightly crunchy texture. Served with parsley buttered new potatoes, Chicken with Dilly Ham Sauce has a tangy breading and savory sauce that's perfect for entertaining…or everyday meals. And impress guests with generous slices of No-Bake Chocolate Torte…it's a no-fuss favorite with lots of flavor!

Chicken with Dilly Ham Sauce

Whether you're preparing a weekday meal or entertaining weekend company, this delicious chicken dish is sure to please. The mustard adds a little "zip", and the ham sauce is a tasty way to top it off.

> 1/2 cup seasoned dry bread crumbs
> 1/2 cup grated Parmesan cheese, *divided*
>   4 boneless skinless chicken breast halves
> 1/3 cup Dijon mustard
> 1/2 cup julienned fully cooked ham (1/4 pound)
>   2 tablespoons butter *or* margarine
>   2 tablespoons all-purpose flour
>   1 cup whipping cream
> 1/2 teaspoon dill weed
> Parsley buttered potatoes, optional

In a shallow dish, combine the bread crumbs and 1/4 cup of the Parmesan cheese; set aside. Pound each chicken breast to 1/4-in. thickness. Brush both sides with mustard; coat evenly with crumb mixture. Place in a greased 13-in. x 9-in. x 2-in. baking pan. Bake, uncovered, at 425° for 15 minutes or until juices run clear. Meanwhile, in a saucepan, saute ham in butter for 2 minutes. Stir in flour until smooth and bubbly. Add cream, dill and remaining Parmesan; cook and stir until thickened and bubbly. Spoon over chicken. Serve with parsley buttered potatoes if desired. **Yield:** 4 servings.

Sesame Asparagus

If you're looking for a unique way to serve asparagus, you'll want to try this tasty dish. Garlic, butter and

chicken broth enhance the delicate flavor of fresh young asparagus in this quick and easy recipe. And sesame seeds add just the right amount of "crunch".

> 1 pound fresh asparagus, cut into 1-1/2-inch pieces (4 cups)
> 1 garlic clove, minced
> 2 tablespoons butter *or* margarine
> 1/2 cup chicken broth
> 1 tablespoon sesame seeds, toasted

In a skillet over medium-high heat, saute the asparagus and garlic in butter for 2 minutes. Stir in broth; bring to a boil. Reduce heat; cover and simmer for 5-6 minutes or until asparagus is crisp-tender. Remove to a serving dish with a slotted spoon; sprinkle with sesame seeds. Serve immediately. **Yield:** 4 servings.

No-Bake Chocolate Torte

Here's a delightful dessert that only looks like you fussed all day. With its attractive appearance and wonderful taste, no one will know that you saved time by spreading an easy-to-prepare frosting on a store-bought pound cake.

1 frozen pound cake (10-3/4 ounces), thawed
2 cups whipping cream
6 tablespoons confectioners' sugar
6 tablespoons baking cocoa
1/2 teaspoon almond extract
1/2 cup sliced almonds, toasted, optional

Slice pound cake lengthwise into three layers and set aside. In a mixing bowl, beat the cream until soft peaks form. Gradually add sugar and cocoa, beat-ing until stiff peaks form. Stir in extract. Frost be-tween cake layers and stack on a serving plate; frost top and sides. Garnish with almonds if desired. Chill at least 15 minutes. Refrigerate any leftovers. **Yield:** 4-6 servings.

Almond Joys

To blanch almonds, cover shelled nuts with boiling water and let stand 3 to 5 minutes. Drain and slide the skins off. Dry on paper towels.

To toast almonds, spread shelled nuts in a shal-low baking pan. Place in a cold oven; toast at 350° for 8 to 12 minutes for whole almonds, stirring occasionally. Remove from pan to cool.

Exciting Outdoor Eating

IT'S TIME to invite family and friends to a potluck in the park. And don't forget the picnic basket brimming with summertime treats! A platterful of tender Broiled Chicken Sandwiches is a great way to greet your hungry guests.

For a cool complement to the meal, dish up some extraordinary Two-Bean Salad. Then add a new twist to a traditional dessert with melt-in-your-mouth Rocky Road Pizza. With great food and good company, everyone will be sad to see the day come to an end. But you can always plan a repeat performance next weekend!

Broiled Chicken Sandwiches

No one will be able to resist these sandwiches, with tender chicken strips tucked into a lightly toasted bun. And in place of traditional mayonnaise or mustard, it features a creamy herbed cheese spread.

- 1 package (3 ounces) cream cheese, softened
- 2 tablespoons butter *or* margarine, softened
- 1/2 teaspoon lemon-pepper seasoning, *divided*
- 1/4 teaspoon dried basil
- 1/8 teaspoon garlic salt
- 1 tablespoon vegetable oil
- 1 tablespoon lemon juice
- 3 to 4 boneless skinless chicken breast halves
- 4 French *or* Italian sandwich rolls, split
- 1 small red onion, sliced

Lettuce leaves

In a small mixing bowl, beat cream cheese, butter, 1/4 teaspoon of lemon pepper, basil and garlic salt until smooth; set aside. Combine oil, lemon juice and remaining lemon pepper. Cut chicken into 1/2-in.-wide strips; brush with lemon juice mixture. Broil chicken 4 in. from the heat for 5 minutes on each side or until juices run clear. Place rolls with cut side up on broiler pan; broil for 1-2 minutes or until light golden brown; spread with the cream cheese mixture. Layer chicken, onion and lettuce over cream cheese. Replace roll tops. **Yield:** 4 servings.

Two-Bean Salad

This simple salad uses frozen and canned beans and prepared salad dressing...so it is extra easy. Assemble this dish and then chill it to have the fabulous flavors blend as you fix the rest of your meal. It's a one-dish delicacy that goes well with many entrees.

- 1 package (10 ounces) frozen cut green beans, thawed
- 1 can (15 ounces) garbanzo beans, rinsed and drained
- 1/3 cup Caesar salad dressing
- 1/4 cup sliced green onions
- 1/4 teaspoon garlic salt

1/8 teaspoon lemon-pepper seasoning

Combine all ingredients in a large bowl. Cover and chill until serving. **Yield:** 4 servings.

———————— ∽⌾∾ ————————

Rocky Road Pizza

Looking for a new, interesting dessert to offer your hungry clan? Chocolate lovers will relish this palate-pleasing pizza that cleverly captures the flavor of rocky road ice cream. Folks will have a hard time eating just one slice!

Pastry for a single-crust pie
  3/4 cup semisweet chocolate chips
  1/2 cup miniature marshmallows
  1/4 cup salted peanuts

Roll pastry into a 9-in. circle; place on a lightly greased baking sheet. Prick with a fork. Bake at 450° for 8-10 minutes or until light brown. Sprinkle with chocolate chips; return to the oven for 1-2 minutes or until chocolate is softened. Spread chocolate out to within 1/2 in. of edges. Sprinkle with marshmallows; return to the oven for 1-2 minutes or until marshmallows puff slightly and are golden brown. Sprinkle with peanuts. Cool. **Yield:** 6-8 servings.

Bountiful Summer Buffet

SUMMERTIME'S in full swing. So why not easily capture the season's terrific tastes with these finger-lickin'-good foods? Pepper Patties tastefully combine colorful peppers, hearty ground beef and tender pasta. Turn your fresh sweet corn into a succulent delight with Spicy Corn Spread. Caramel ice cream topping enhances the natural sweetness of fruits in Strawberry Kiwi Dessert.

Pepper Patties

Bring the season's taste inside by fixing skillet-fried beef burgers and colorful peppers. The serving suggestions are many—present them on a bed of hot cooked noodles for a hearty dinner, alone for a lighter meal or on bread as an open-faced sandwich.

> 2 tablespoons soy sauce
> 1/4 teaspoon garlic powder
> 1/4 teaspoon pepper
> 1 pound ground beef
> 1 teaspoon vegetable oil
> 1 small onion, sliced
> 1 small green pepper, julienned
> 1 small sweet red pepper, julienned

Hot cooked noodles, optional

In a medium bowl, combine soy sauce, garlic powder and pepper; place 1 tablespoon in a large skillet and set aside. Add beef to remaining soy sauce mixture; mix well. Shape into four 1/2-in.-thick patties. Add oil to the skillet; heat on medium. Add onion and peppers; cook and stir for 3-4 minutes or until crisp-tender. Remove and set aside. Add patties to skillet; cook for 3 minutes on each side or until beef is no longer pink. Top patties with peppers and onion; heat through. Serve over noodles if desired. **Yield:** 4 servings.

Spicy Corn Spread

This specially seasoned spread won't only add "kick" to corn on the cob, it'll "zip up" zucchini or any other cooked vegetables. If you like, you can adapt the recipe to suit your family's tastes by adjusting the amount of chili powder.

> 1/4 cup butter *or* margarine, softened
> 1/2 teaspoon dried parsley flakes
> 1/4 teaspoon chili powder
> 1/4 teaspoon salt

Hot cooked corn on the cob

In a small bowl, combine the butter, parsley, chili powder and salt until smooth. Spread on hot ears of corn. Refrigerate any leftovers. **Yield:** 4 servings.

Strawberry Kiwi Dessert

In the heat of summer, folks will look forward to a light dessert like this. The season's finest fruits are slightly sweetened with caramel, orange juice and honey. Serve this fruity finale alone or as a topping on other favorite desserts.

 3 cups halved fresh strawberries
 2 kiwifruit, peeled and sliced

 2 tablespoons caramel ice cream topping
 1 tablespoon orange juice
 2 to 3 tablespoons honey roasted almonds *or* toasted almonds

Place fruit in a serving bowl. Combine caramel topping and orange juice; drizzle over fruit. Sprinkle with nuts. **Yield:** 4 servings. **Editor's Note:** May also be served over angel food cake, pound cake or ice cream.

Quick-and-Easy Cookout Cuisine

WHEN WARM WEATHER comes your way, it's time to fire up the grill for an old-fashioned country-style barbecue. Nothing says "Summer!" quite like sizzling juicy Mushroom Cheeseburgers. Busy cooks will appreciate that kitchen mess is kept to a minimum with Grilled Parmesan Potatoes. Ruby-red homegrown tomatoes make Italian Tomato Salad an extra-special addition to any meal.

Mushroom Cheeseburgers

Instead of topping juicy cheeseburgers with sauteed mushrooms, include some in the meat mixture for a new twist! Folks will be pleasantly surprised with these deluxe sandwiches...bite after bite.

  1/4 **cup chopped canned mushrooms**
  1/4 **cup finely chopped onion**
    1 **teaspoon dried oregano**
  1/2 **teaspoon salt**
  1/2 **teaspoon pepper**
    1 **pound ground beef**
    4 **slices process American cheese**
    4 **hamburger buns, split**
Lettuce leaves, optional

In a medium bowl, combine the mushrooms, onion, oregano, salt and pepper; add beef and mix well. Shape into four patties. Grill burgers, uncovered, over medium-hot heat for 5-6 minutes on each side or until no longer pink. Top each burger with a slice of cheese. Serve on buns with lettuce if desired. **Yield:** 4 servings.

Grilled Parmesan Potatoes

Take a break from usual baked potatoes—and keep the oven cool in the meantime—by cooking these spectacular "spuds" on the grill. Since there's no need to boil the potatoes ahead of time, this tasty, no-fuss favorite is sure to become a timeless classic in your recipe collection.

☑ Uses less fat, sugar or salt. Includes Nutritional Analysis and Diabetic Exchanges.

    1 **pound small red potatoes**

  1/4 **cup chopped green onions**
    2 **teaspoons vegetable oil**
    1 **tablespoon grated Parmesan cheese**
    1 **teaspoon dried oregano**
  1/2 **teaspoon garlic salt**
  1/4 **teaspoon pepper**

Cut potatoes into 1/2-in. cubes; place in a medium bowl. Add onions and oil; toss to coat. Place in the center of a large piece of heavy-duty aluminum foil (about 18 in. x 12 in.). Combine Parmesan cheese, oregano, garlic salt and pepper; sprinkle over potato mixture. Fold foil into a pouch and seal tightly. Grill, uncoverd, over medium-hot heat for 18-20 minutes or until potatoes are tender. Open

foil carefully to allow steam to escape. **Yield:** 4 servings. **Nutritional Analysis:** One serving equals 104 calories, 200 mg sodium, 1 mg cholesterol, 16 gm carbohydrate, 3 gm protein, 3 gm fat. **Diabetic Exchanges:** 1 starch, 1/2 fat.

Italian Tomato Salad

When sharing your bumper crop of tomatoes with friends, be sure to send along a copy of this extra-easy recipe. The light oil-and-vinegar dressing and subtle seasonings let the wonderful flavors of just-picked tomatoes and crisp cucumbers come through.

> 2 **medium tomatoes, sliced**
> 1/2 **medium cucumber, sliced**
> 1 **small red onion, thinly sliced**
> 1/4 **cup vegetable oil**
> 2 **tablespoons cider *or* red wine vinegar**
> 2 **tablespoons chopped fresh basil *or* 2 teaspoons dried basil**
> 1/4 **teaspoon salt**
> 1/8 **teaspoon pepper**

Layer tomatoes, cucumber and onion in a large salad bowl. Combine oil, vinegar, basil, salt and pepper; drizzle over vegetables. Cover and refrigerate until serving. **Yield:** 4 servings.

Classic Comfort Foods Will Warm the Spirit in Fall

TRICK-OR-TREATING FARE will be forgotten when you set these comforting foods on the table. Preparing them will be a real treat for you, since they can be ready in under half an hour!

Tangy Beef Stroganoff, from Rita Farmer of Houston, Texas, is a rich, comforting main dish that tastes like you were in the kitchen all day.

"Now that I'm retired, I'm busy taking computer classes and helping out at church," relates Rita. "When I want to treat my daughter and her family to a meal, this dish is quick and delicious."

Crumb-Topped Brussels Sprouts get a tasty Parmesan cheese topping in the recipe sent by Ruth Peterson of Jenison, Michigan.

Says Mary Brenneman of Tavistock, Ontario, "Microwave Chocolate Cake is a wonderfully versatile cake I've made many times."

Tangy Beef Stroganoff

   1 **pound sirloin steak**
1/4 **cup butter *or* margarine**
   8 **ounces fresh mushrooms, sliced**
1/2 **cup sliced onion**
   1 **garlic clove, minced**
   2 **tablespoons all-purpose flour**
   1 **cup water**
   1 **tablespoon lemon juice**
   1 **tablespoon cider *or* red wine vinegar**
   2 **teaspoons beef bouillon granules**
1/2 **teaspoon salt**
1/4 **teaspoon pepper**
   1 **cup (8 ounces) sour cream**
Hot cooked noodles
Chopped fresh parsley and paprika, optional

Cut beef into 1/8-in.-thick strips. In a large skillet over medium-high heat, cook beef in butter until no longer pink. Remove with a slotted spoon and keep warm. In the pan juices, cook mushrooms, onion and garlic until tender; stir in flour. Add water, lemon juice, vinegar, bouillon, salt and pepper; bring to a boil. Cook and stir for 2 minutes. Stir in sour cream and beef; heat through but do not boil. Serve over noodles. Garnish with parsley and paprika if desired. **Yield:** 4 servings.

Crumb-Topped Brussels Sprouts

1-1/2 **pounds fresh *or* frozen brussels sprouts**
   3 **tablespoons butter *or* margarine, melted**
1/4 **cup Italian-seasoned dry bread crumbs**
   2 **tablespoons grated Parmesan cheese**

In a saucepan, cook brussels sprouts in salted water until crisp-tender, about 8-10 minutes; drain. Place in an ungreased shallow 1-1/2-qt. baking dish. Drizzle with 2 tablespoons butter. Combine remaining butter, bread crumbs and Parmesan cheese; sprinkle over brussels sprouts. Cover and bake at 325° for 10 minutes. Uncover and bake 10 minutes longer. **Yield:** 4-6 servings.

Microwave Chocolate Cake

1-1/2 **cups all-purpose flour**
   1 **cup sugar**
   3 **tablespoons baking cocoa**
   1 **teaspoon baking soda**
1/4 **teaspoon salt**
   1 **cup cold water**
1/3 **cup vegetable oil**
   1 **tablespoon vinegar**
   1 **teaspoon vanilla extract**
CHOCOLATE SAUCE:
   1 **cup sugar**
   3 **tablespoons cornstarch**
   2 **tablespoons baking cocoa**
   1 **cup boiling water**
Dash salt
   1 **tablespoon butter *or* margarine**
   1 **teaspoon vanilla extract**

In a bowl, combine the first five ingredients. Stir in water, oil, vinegar and vanilla until well blended. Pour into an ungreased 8-in. square microwave-safe dish. Microwave on high for 6-8 minutes, turning dish every 2 minutes, or until a toothpick inserted near the center comes out clean. In a 1-qt. microwave-safe bowl, combine sugar, cornstarch and cocoa. Stir in water and salt. Microwave on high for 2-3 minutes, stirring occasionally, or until mixture boils. Microwave 1 minute more. Stir in butter and vanilla. Spoon over pieces of warm cake. **Yield:** 9 servings. **Editor's Note:** This recipe was tested in a 700-watt microwave.

Mmmm-Morning Meal

NOTHING STARTS your day off right like a down-home country breakfast featuring a Fluffy Harvest Omelet that's chock-full of fresh vegetables and cheese. Your family will be delighted when you serve their favorite fruit in Honey Fruit Cups. And Simple Pecan Rolls use prepackaged buns so they bake up to a sweet and sticky golden brown in just minutes.

Fluffy Harvest Omelet

With its mushrooms, zucchini and tomato sauce, this hearty omelet isn't just for breakfast. Your family will savor it as a change-of-pace lunch or dinner, too.

  6 eggs, *separated*
1/4 teaspoon salt
1/4 cup half-and-half cream
1/4 cup grated Parmesan cheese
1/4 teaspoon pepper
  2 tablespoons butter *or* margarine
  1 can (15 ounces) chunky Italian tomato sauce
  1 cup cubed fresh zucchini
3/4 cup sliced fresh mushrooms
  1 cup (4 ounces) shredded mozzarella cheese

In a large mixing bowl, beat egg whites until soft peaks form. Add salt; continue beating until stiff peaks form. In a small mixing bowl, beat the egg yolks, cream, Parmesan cheese and pepper until foamy. Gently fold into the egg whites. Melt butter in a 10-in. ovenproof skillet; add egg mixture. Cook over medium-low heat for 8 minutes or until bottom is golden brown. Place skillet in a 350° oven for 10 minutes or until top is golden brown. Meanwhile, combine the tomato sauce, zucchini and mushrooms in a small saucepan. Cook, uncovered, until zucchini is tender, about 10 minutes. Sprinkle mozzarella cheese over omelet; fold in half and top with tomato sauce. **Yield:** 4 servings.

Basil Makes It Better
Basil adds great flavor to scrambled eggs, salads and buttered noodles.

Honey Fruit Cups

For a naturally sweet addition to your meal, combine your family's favorite fruits and top with a refreshing honey-yogurt sauce. It'll disappear fast!

  4 cups cut-up fresh fruit (pears, apples, bananas, grapes, etc.)
  1 carton (6 ounces) mandarin orange, vanilla *or* lemon yogurt
  1 tablespoon honey
1/2 teaspoon grated orange peel
1/4 teaspoon almond extract

Divide fruit among individual serving bowls. Combine yogurt, honey, orange peel and extract; spoon over the fruit. **Yield:** 4 servings.

Simple Pecan Rolls

There's no letting the dough rise overnight with these delightful cinnamon pecan rolls...all you need is a package of ready-made rolls. It can stay your secret that these sticky treats weren't made from scratch!

1/2 cup butter *or* margarine, softened
1/2 cup packed brown sugar
1/2 teaspoon ground cinnamon
3/4 cup pecan halves
  1 package (12 count) brown-and-serve rolls

In a mixing bowl, beat butter, brown sugar and cinnamon until well blended. Spread in the bottom of a 9-in. round baking pan. Top with pecans. Place rolls upside down over pecans. Bake at 450° for 8-10 minutes or until golden. Immediately turn onto a serving platter. Serve warm. **Yield:** 4-6 servings.

Festive Fall Fare

COUNTRY COOKS know that cool autumn air calls for plenty of flavorful family-style suppers. Folks will find the aroma of stick-to-the-ribs Harvest Pork Chops irresistible, while Skillet Ranch Vegetables splendidly showcase the last of your garden's goodness. Then head to the orchard and select some of fall's finest fruit for sweet Honey-Nut Apples.

Harvest Pork Chops

Cooks agree the very best recipes are fast, flavorful and versatile! These tender pork chops are quickly browned, then popped into the oven. For a casual dinner, present each guest with an individual packet. Or unwrap the chops and present on a pretty platter.

    1/2 teaspoon salt
    1/4 teaspoon pepper
    1/4 teaspoon paprika
    1/4 teaspoon rubbed sage
    1/4 teaspoon dried thyme
      4 boneless loin pork chops (1/2 inch thick)
      1 tablespoon vegetable oil
      1 small onion, sliced

Combine salt, pepper, paprika, sage and thyme; sprinkle over both sides of pork chops. In a skillet, brown chops in oil for 1-2 minutes on each side. Place each chop in the center of a large piece of heavy-duty aluminum foil (about 12 in. x 9 in.). Top with onion slices. Seal foil tightly; place pouches on a baking sheet. Bake at 450° for 25 minutes or until meat is no longer pink. Open foil carefully to allow steam to escape. **Yield:** 4 servings.

Skillet Ranch Vegetables

Celebrate the last garden harvest with this satisfying side dish. Simply cook carrots, squash and zucchini in oil that's been spiced up with ranch dressing mix. You'll be able to dish out hot and hearty helpings in minutes!

      1 tablespoon vegetable oil
      1 envelope buttermilk ranch salad
        dressing mix
      2 medium carrots, thinly sliced
      2 medium yellow squash, sliced
      2 medium zucchini, sliced

In a skillet, combine the oil and salad dressing mix. Add carrots; cook over medium heat for 4-5 minutes or until crisp-tender. Add squash and zucchini; cook 4-5 minutes longer or until all of the vegetables are tender. Remove with a slotted spoon to serving dish. **Yield:** 4 servings.

Honey-Nut Apples

When apples are ripe for the picking, you're bound to get many requests for this tempting treat. It's a fun, festive way to bring a fall feel to your table.

2 tablespoons butter *or* margarine
2 tablespoons brown sugar
1/8 teaspoon ground cinnamon

3 large tart apples, thickly sliced
1/4 cup chopped walnuts
1 tablespoon honey

Melt butter in a large skillet over medium heat. Stir in brown sugar and cinnamon. Add apples and walnuts. Cook, stirring occasionally, for 8-10 minutes or until tender. Remove from the heat and drizzle with honey. Serve warm. **Yield:** 4 servings.

Take Stock in Festive No-Fuss Treat

WITH CARDS to send, a tree to trim and presents to wrap, who has time to spend hours in the kitchen during the holiday season? This satisfying quick meal may be just the gift to give yourself and your family!

The complete-meal menu here is made up of favorite recipes shared by three great cooks and combined in the *Taste of Home* Test Kitchen. You can have everything ready to serve in just half an hour.

Chicken Crescent Wreath is an impressive-looking main dish that's a snap to prepare. "Even when my cooking time is limited, I can still serve this delicious wreath," says Marlene Denissen of Maplewood, Minnesota. "The red pepper and green broccoli add a festive touch."

Parmesan Buttered Rice is recommended by Rose Marie Dama of Waco, Texas. "The flavorful and simple butter, Parmesan cheese and parsley topping gives plain rice a tasty twist the whole family enjoys," Rose Marie assures.

"Fruit and Cream Parfaits are lovely and special desserts that look fussy but are really easy to fix," says Jeannette Mack of Rushville, New York. "I've also made them using other pie fillings like strawberry, raspberry and blueberry."

Chicken Crescent Wreath

- 2 tubes (8 ounces *each*) refrigerated crescent rolls
- 1 cup (4 ounces) shredded Co-Jack cheese
- 2/3 cup condensed cream of chicken soup, undiluted
- 1/2 cup chopped fresh broccoli
- 1/2 cup chopped sweet red pepper
- 1/4 cup chopped water chestnuts
- 1 can (5 ounces) white chicken, drained *or* 3/4 cup cubed cooked chicken
- 2 tablespoons chopped onion

Arrange the crescent rolls on a 12-in. pizza pan, forming a ring with pointed ends facing the outer edge of pan and wide ends overlapping. Combine the remaining ingredients; spoon over wide ends of rolls. Fold points over filling and tuck under wide ends (filling will be visible). Bake at 375° for 20-25 minutes or until golden brown. **Yield:** 6-8 servings.

Parmesan Buttered Rice

- 3 cups water
- 1-1/2 cups uncooked long grain rice
- 1/2 cup butter (no substitutes)
- 1-1/2 cups grated Parmesan cheese
- 1 tablespoon minced fresh parsley

In a large saucepan, bring water to a boil; stir in rice. Reduce heat to low; cover and cook for 20 minutes or until tender. Meanwhile, in a skillet over medium heat, melt butter until browned. Place rice in a serving dish; sprinkle with Parmesan cheese. Pour butter over rice; cover and let stand for 2-3 minutes. Sprinkle with parsley. **Yield:** 6-8 servings.

Fruit and Cream Parfaits

- 1 cup whipping cream
- 3 tablespoons sugar
- 1 teaspoon vanilla extract
- Dash salt
- 1 cup (8 ounces) sour cream
- 1 can (21 ounces) cherry, strawberry, raspberry *or* blueberry pie filling, *divided*

In a mixing bowl, whip cream until soft peaks form. Gradually add sugar, vanilla and salt; beat until stiff peaks form. Fold in sour cream. Set aside six cherries from pie filling. Spoon half of the remaining pie filling into parfait glasses; top with half of the cream mixture. Repeat layers. Top with reserved cherries. **Yield:** 6 servings.

Rapid Recipes with Rice

Cooked rice can be stored in the refrigerator for up to 1 week and in the freezer for up to 6 months. So you can cook rice in double batches to have some on hand for making quick meals.

Leftovers make great fried rice. Just saute in a small amount of oil with chopped green onions or mushrooms. Or combine leftover rice, sliced bananas and a can of crushed pineapple for an easy dessert.

Soup-and-Sandwich Duo Always Delights

THE CLASSIC combination of soup and a sandwich makes a comforting and versatile meal. It's a dynamite duo that busy cooks across the country can turn to time and time again.

The soup and sandwich meal here is made up of family favorites from three great cooks. You can have everything ready to serve in only 30 minutes.

Cheeseburger Loaf is a satisfying quick main dish that Brenda Rohlman remembers her mom making years ago. "I sometimes use spaghetti sauce with mozzarella cheese or picante sauce with Monterey Jack cheese to vary the taste," says this Kingman, Kansas cook.

Zesty Potato Soup is suggested by Marsha Benda of Round Rock, Texas, who says, "This creamy soup has a delightful zip that sparks recipe requests. Folks love the combination of potatoes, cheese and green chilies. It's a nice change of pace from regular potato soup."

Butterscotch Pecan Cookies have a rich buttery flavor. "No one will guess they started from convenient cake and pudding mixes," assures Betty Janway of Ruston, Louisiana. "I make a batch even when I do have time to spare."

Cheeseburger Loaf

    1 pound ground beef
1/4 cup chopped onion
    1 can (10-3/4 ounces) condensed tomato
        soup, undiluted
1/2 teaspoon garlic salt
1/4 teaspoon salt
1/4 teaspoon pepper
    1 loaf (1 pound) French bread
    1 tablespoon butter *or* margarine,
        softened
    8 ounces process American *or* Mexican-
        flavored cheese, sliced

In a saucepan over medium heat, cook beef and onion until meat is no longer pink; drain. Add soup, garlic salt, salt and pepper; simmer for 5-10 minutes. Meanwhile, slice the top third off the bread. Hollow out bottom half of loaf, leaving a 3/4-in. shell (discard removed bread or save for another use). Spread butter on cut side of bread. Place loaf on a baking sheet and broil until lightly browned. Spoon beef mixture into shell; arrange cheese slices on top. Broil until cheese is melted, about 2-3 minutes. Replace bread top. **Yield:** 6-8 servings.

Zesty Potato Soup

    4 large potatoes, peeled and cubed
    2 cups water
    1 teaspoon dried minced onion
    1 garlic clove, minced
1/2 teaspoon salt
1/4 teaspoon pepper
    1 cup milk
    4 ounces process American cheese, cubed
1/3 cup chopped green chilies
    2 tablespoons butter *or* margarine
    1 tablespoon chicken bouillon granules
    2 teaspoons minced fresh parsley

In a large saucepan, combine the potatoes, water, onion, garlic, salt and pepper; bring to a boil over medium heat. Reduce heat; cover and simmer for 15-20 minutes or until potatoes are tender. (Do not drain.) Mash potatoes in liquid until almost smooth. Add remaining ingredients; cook and stir until the cheese is melted. **Yield:** 6 servings.

Butterscotch Pecan Cookies

    1 package (18-1/4 ounces) butter recipe
        cake mix*
    1 package (3.4 ounces) instant butterscotch
        pudding mix
1/4 cup all-purpose flour
3/4 cup vegetable oil
    1 egg
    1 cup chopped pecans

In a mixing bowl, combine the first five ingredients and mix well. Stir in pecans (the dough will be crumbly). Roll tablespoonfuls into balls; place 2 in. apart on greased baking sheets. Bake at 350° for 10-12 minutes or until golden brown. Cool for 2 minutes; remove from pans to wire racks. **Yield:** 4 dozen. ***Editor's Note:** This recipe was tested with Pillsbury brand butter recipe cake mix.

Hearty Ham Dinner's Ready in a Hurry

FOR THOSE who love to cook, spending time in the kitchen preparing an elaborate meal is a joy. Still, there are some days when you need to pull together a satisfying meal in just minutes.

The fast and flavorful meal here is made up of tried-and-true favorites from three busy cooks. You can have everything on the table in just half an hour!

Hurry-Up Ham 'n' Noodles is a rich-tasting entree created by Lucille Howell of Portland, Oregon. "This basic hearty dish is ready to serve in almost the time it takes to cook the noodles," she says. "I make it often for luncheons and potlucks. Mostly I make it on days when I'm in a hurry to get something on the table."

Continues Lucille, "This stovetop specialty is a great way to use up leftover ham from Easter, Christmas or any other dinner."

Tangy Carrot Coins give a popular nutritious vegetable a new twist, remarks Lois Stephen from Mt. Morris, Michigan. "This colorful side dish is as easy to fix as plain carrots, but the light, creamy coating makes them extra yummy," she adds. "Even folks who don't usually care for carrots gobble them up in no time…then ask for more!"

Peachy Sundaes are a treat grandmother Betty Claycomb has enjoyed since she was a teenager. "Years ago, a friend worked at a fancy hotel where this deliciously different dessert was served," recalls this Alverton, Pennsylvania cook. "These sundaes are very simple to prepare but look and taste elegant."

Hurry-Up Ham 'n' Noodles

    5 to 6 cups uncooked wide egg noodles
  1/4 cup butter *or* margarine
    1 cup whipping cream
1-1/2 cups julienned fully cooked ham
  1/2 cup grated Parmesan cheese
  1/4 cup thinly sliced green onions
  1/4 teaspoon salt
  1/8 teaspoon pepper

Cook noodles according to package directions. Meanwhile, in a skillet over medium heat, melt butter. Stir in cream. Bring to a boil; cook and stir for 2 minutes. Add ham, cheese, onions, salt and pepper; heat through. Drain noodles; add to ham mixture and heat through. **Yield:** 4 servings.

Tangy Carrot Coins

    1 pound carrots, sliced
    3 tablespoons butter *or* margarine
    1 tablespoon brown sugar
    1 tablespoon Dijon mustard
  1/8 teaspoon salt

Place carrots in a saucepan. Add 1 in. of water; bring to a boil. Reduce heat; cover and simmer for 7-9 minutes or until crisp-tender. Drain. Add the butter, brown sugar, Dijon mustard and salt; cook and stir over medium heat for 1-2 minutes or until sauce is thickened and carrots are coated. **Yield:** 4 servings.

Peachy Sundaes

    1 pint vanilla ice cream
  1/2 to 1 cup peach preserves, warmed
  1/4 cup chopped almonds, toasted
  1/4 cup flaked coconut, toasted, optional

Divide ice cream among four individual dishes. Top with preserves; sprinkle with almonds and coconut if desired. **Yield:** 4 servings.

A Bunch of Carrot Tips

The best carrots are young and slender. Look for those that are firm and smooth; avoid any with cracks or that have begun to soften and wither.

If buying carrots with their greenery, make sure the leaves are moist and bright green. Carrot greens rob the roots of moisture and vitamins, so remove them as soon as you get home.

Store carrots in a plastic bag in the refrigerator for up to 2 weeks.

Scrumptious Stroganoff Is a Festive Feast

DURING THE SEASON of shopping for the perfect present, wouldn't it be great to give yourself the gift of time?

Consider it done. This warm and satisfying meal will please your family without taking much time away from your holiday to-do list.

Your family will love the way it tastes, and you'll love the fact that it's quick and easy to prepare. From start to finish, it takes only 30 minutes.

The menu is made up of favorite recipes shared by three accomplished cooks and combined in the *Taste of Home* Test Kitchen.

Mushroom Beef Stroganoff is a tried-and-true dish that is nice enough for company, says Robin De La Gardelle of Concord, California.

"I've had this recipe for more than 25 years and have used it countless times," she says. "You can serve it over noodles or rice."

Herbed Tossed Salad is a fresh-tasting side dish from Margery Bryan of Royal City, Washington. The sweet red pepper gives it crunch, spark and a festive appearance.

Candy Bar Croissants taste as good as they look. This rich, buttery treat combines convenient refrigerated crescent rolls and chocolate bars. The recipe comes from Beverly Sterling of Gasport, New York.

Mushroom Beef Stroganoff

2 tablespoons butter *or* margarine
1 tablespoon vegetable oil
1-1/2 pounds sirloin steak, thinly sliced
1 pound fresh mushrooms, sliced
1 can (10-3/4 ounces) condensed cream of mushroom soup, undiluted
2 cups (16 ounces) sour cream
1 cup chopped green onions
1/2 teaspoon dried thyme
1/2 teaspoon dried marjoram
Hot cooked noodles *or* rice

In a large skillet, heat butter and oil over medium-high heat. Brown steak; remove with a slotted spoon and keep warm. Add mushrooms; saute until tender. Return steak to pan. Add soup, sour cream, onions, thyme and marjoram; heat gently (do not boil). Serve over noodles or rice. **Yield:** 6 servings.

Herbed Tossed Salad

1 cup vegetable oil
1/3 cup tarragon *or* cider vinegar
1 garlic clove, minced
2 teaspoons minced fresh oregano *or* 1/2 teaspoon dried oregano
1 teaspoon salt
3/4 to 1 teaspoon minced fresh basil *or* 1/4 teaspoon dried basil
1/2 teaspoon minced fresh parsley
Mixed salad greens
Sliced cucumber and sweet red pepper

In a jar with a tight-fitting lid, combine the first seven ingredients; shake well. In a large salad bowl, combine greens, cucumber and red pepper. Drizzle with dressing; toss to coat. **Yield:** about 1-1/3 cups dressing.

Candy Bar Croissants

1 tube (8 ounces) refrigerated crescent rolls
1 tablespoon butter *or* margarine, softened
2 plain milk chocolate candy bars (1.55 ounces *each*), broken into small pieces
1 egg, beaten
2 tablespoons sliced almonds

Unroll crescent roll dough; separate into triangles. Brush with butter. Arrange candy bar pieces evenly over triangles; roll up from the wide end. Place point side down on a greased baking sheet; curve ends slightly. Brush with egg and sprinkle with almonds. Bake at 375° for 11-13 minutes or until golden brown. Cool on a wire rack. **Yield:** 8 servings.

A Sure Thyme-Saver

Dry thyme by hanging bunches of stems secured with a rubber band in a warm dark area. Strip the dried leaves off by running your forefinger and thumb down each stem over a piece of paper. Slide the leaves into an air-tight container. Fresh thyme, which also freezes very well, is great on vegetables as well as poultry and all meats, game and fish.

Chicken Salad Brings Cool Refreshment

THE SEASON helps determine how much time is spent in the kitchen. A clear summer day tempts even the most avid cooks to minimize time there.

This menu will give you plenty of time to garden, swim or enjoy a host of other outdoor activities. Its cool and creamy components will provide a welcome chill on a scorching day. Truly, though, it's a refreshing meal any time of year.

The menu was created in our Test Kitchen using tried-and-true recipes from three seasoned cooks. You can put together this complete meal—including dessert—in 30 minutes or less.

Dijon Chicken Salad is a tasty combination from Raymond Sienko of Hawleyville, Connecticut. "This is, by far, my most requested recipe," he says. "In addition to the traditional grapes, this chicken salad also features sweet apricots."

Buttermilk Rosemary Muffins have a delicate herb flavor that's special alongside any entree. Here, it complements the chicken salad especially well. The recipe is from Debbie Smith of Crossett, Arkansas, who suggests using fresh rosemary for best flavor.

Butterscotch Parfaits, from Judi Klee of Nebraska City, Nebraska, are pretty confections that are impossible to turn down. "Change the pudding flavor to suit your tastes," suggests Judi.

Dijon Chicken Salad

4 cups cubed cooked chicken
1 cup sliced celery
1 cup seedless green grapes, halved
1 cup seedless red grapes, halved
1/4 cup chopped dried apricots
1/4 cup sliced green onions
3/4 cup mayonnaise
2 tablespoons honey
1 tablespoon Dijon mustard
1/2 teaspoon salt
1/8 teaspoon pepper
Lettuce leaves
1/2 cup sliced almonds

In a bowl, combine the first six ingredients. In a small bowl, combine the mayonnaise, honey, mustard, salt and pepper; mix well. Stir into chicken mixture. Cover and refrigerate until serving. Serve on a lettuce-lined plate. Sprinkle with the almonds. **Yield:** 6 servings.

Buttermilk Rosemary Muffins

2-1/4 cups all-purpose flour
2 tablespoons sugar
1 tablespoon baking powder
2 teaspoons minced fresh rosemary *or* 3/4 teaspoon dried rosemary, crushed
3/4 teaspoon salt
1/2 cup plus 1 tablespoon shortening
3/4 cup buttermilk
1/4 cup butter *or* margarine, melted

In a large bowl, combine the first five ingredients. Cut in shortening until mixture resembles coarse crumbs. Stir in buttermilk just until moistened (mixture will be dry). Fill greased muffin cups two-thirds full; brush with butter. Bake at 400° for 10-13 minutes or until a toothpick comes out clean. Cool for 5 minutes before removing from pan to a wire rack. Serve warm. **Yield:** 1 dozen.

Butterscotch Parfaits

 Uses less fat, sugar or salt. Includes Nutritional Analysis and Diabetic Exchanges.

2 cups cold milk
1 package (3.4 ounces) instant butterscotch pudding mix
18 vanilla wafers, coarsely crushed
1 carton (8 ounces) frozen whipped topping, thawed
6 maraschino cherries, optional

In a mixing bowl, beat milk and pudding mix for 2 minutes or until thickened. In six parfait glasses, alternate layers of pudding, wafer crumbs and whipped topping. Garnish with a cherry if desired. Refrigerate until serving. **Yield:** 6 servings. **Nutritional Analysis:** One serving (prepared with skim milk, instant sugar-free pudding mix and light whipped topping and without cherries) equals 194 calories, 289 mg sodium, 2 mg cholesterol, 25 gm carbohydrate, 4 gm protein, 7 gm fat, 0 fiber. **Diabetic Exchanges:** 2 starch, 1/2 fat.

Chicken and Asparagus Dinner in a Snap

IT WOULD BE so wonderful if every family meal could be an elaborate spread. But when reality comes knocking at your door and you need to get a meal on the table in minutes instead of hours, here's a menu to reach for.

This complete meal is made up of family favorites shared by three great cooks and combined in our Test Kitchen. You can have everything on your table in only 30 minutes.

Crispy Chicken Cutlets are moist and tender with a golden nutty coating. They go especially well with egg noodles.

"This is an easy entree I proudly serve to company," says Debra Smith of Brookfield, Missouri. "Try it for your next spur-of-the-moment dinner party or family dinner. Even your most finicky eater will be singing its praises—and yours!"

Stir-Fried Asparagus is a fresh-tasting, nicely seasoned vegetable side dish that's a cinch to prepare. The recipe, from Jeanette Lawrence of Vacaville, California, puts to good use those tender, garden-fresh asparagus of springtime.

Honey Peach Freeze makes a cool, refreshing end to any meal. The tang of orange and lemon juice blends nicely with the honey. It's great for anyone who is on a restricted diet, and those who aren't won't know the difference.

"This lightly sweet treat has big peach flavor," says Dorothy Smith of El Dorado, Arkansas.

Crispy Chicken Cutlets

    4 boneless skinless chicken breast halves
    1 egg white
3/4 cup finely chopped pecans
    3 tablespoons all-purpose flour
1/4 teaspoon salt
1/4 teaspoon pepper
    1 tablespoon butter *or* margarine
    1 tablespoon vegetable oil

Flatten chicken to 1/4-in. thickness. In a shallow bowl, lightly beat the egg white. In another shallow bowl, combine the pecans, flour, salt and pepper. Dip chicken in egg white, then coat with the pecan mixture. In a large skillet, brown chicken in butter and oil over medium heat for 4-6 minutes on each side or until juices run clear. **Yield:** 4 servings.

Stir-Fried Asparagus

    3 tablespoons butter *or* margarine
    1 teaspoon chicken bouillon granules
1/8 teaspoon celery salt
1/8 teaspoon pepper
1-1/2 pounds fresh asparagus, trimmed and cut
        into 2-inch slices (about 4 cups)
    1 teaspoon soy sauce

In a large skillet, melt butter. Add bouillon, celery salt and pepper; mix well. Add asparagus and toss to coat. Cover and cook for 2 minutes over medium-high heat, stirring occasionally. Stir in soy sauce and serve immediately. **Yield:** 4 servings.

Honey Peach Freeze

✓ Uses less fat, sugar or salt. Includes Nutritional Analysis and Diabetic Exchanges.

    1 package (20 ounces) frozen sliced
        peaches, partially thawed
1/4 cup honey
    2 tablespoons orange juice
    1 tablespoon lemon juice

Set aside a few peach slices for garnish if desired. Place remaining peaches in a blender or food processor; add honey and juices. Cover and process until smooth. Pour into four freezer-proof dishes. Freeze. Remove from the freezer 5 minutes before serving. Garnish with reserved peaches. **Yield:** 4 servings. **Nutritional Analysis:** One serving equals 202 calories, 9 mg sodium, 0 cholesterol, 53 gm carbohydrate, 1 gm protein, trace fat, 3 gm fiber. **Diabetic Exchange:** 3-1/2 fruit.

Juicy Tidbits

Need to quickly prepare juice from a can of frozen concentrate? Slide the frozen concentrate into a pitcher, then mash it with a potato masher. It will dissolve in water a lot faster.

Use orange juice for the liquid in homemade waffle batter. It gives the waffles a sweet citrus flavor your breakfast bunch is sure to love.

Summer Meal Adds Some Sizzle to Supper

SPICE UP your summer meal without turning up the heat in the kitchen. With this Southwestern-style meal, you'll be out of the kitchen in less than 30 minutes!

It's a complete-meal menu made up of favorites from three great cooks, combined in our Test Kitchen.

Chicken Quesadillas have an impressive look and taste with little preparation. "Leftover chicken gets Mexican flair from cumin in this fun main dish," says Linda Wetzel of Woodland Park, Colorado.

"Zippy Beans and Rice is a super side dish, and we also enjoy it as a light entree with corn bread and salad," shares Darlene Owen of Reedsport, Oregon.

Berry Pineapple Parfaits from Ruth Andrewson of Peck, Idaho are lovely and refreshing.

Chicken Quesadillas

2-1/2 cups shredded cooked chicken
2/3 cup salsa
1/3 cup sliced green onions
3/4 to 1 teaspoon ground cumin
1/2 teaspoon salt
1/2 teaspoon dried oregano
6 flour tortillas (8 inches)
1/4 cup butter or margarine, melted
2 cups (8 ounces) shredded Monterey Jack cheese
Sour cream and guacamole

In a skillet, combine the first six ingredients. Cook, uncovered, over medium heat for 10 minutes or until heated through, stirring occasionally. Brush one side of tortillas with butter. Spoon 1/3 cup chicken mixture over half of unbuttered side of each tortilla. Sprinkle with 1/3 cup cheese; fold plain side of tortilla over cheese. Place on a lightly greased baking sheet. Bake at 475° for 10 minutes or until crisp and golden brown. Cut into wedges; serve with sour cream and guacamole. **Yield:** 6 servings.

Zippy Beans and Rice

✓ Uses less fat, sugar or salt. Includes Nutritional Analysis and Diabetic Exchanges.

1 can (15 ounces) black beans, rinsed and drained

1 can (10 ounces) diced tomatoes and green chilies, undrained
1 cup frozen corn
3/4 cup water
1 medium jalapeno pepper, seeded and chopped*
1 teaspoon salt, optional
1 cup uncooked instant white or brown rice
1 green onion, sliced

In a skillet, combine the beans, tomatoes, corn, water, jalapeno and salt if desired. Bring to a boil; stir in rice. Cover and remove from the heat. Let stand for 5 minutes or until liquid is absorbed. Sprinkle with onion. **Yield:** 6 servings. **Nutritional Analysis:** One 3/4-cup serving (prepared with brown rice and without salt) equals 197 calories, 414 mg sodium, 0 cholesterol, 40 gm carbohydrate, 8 gm protein, 2 gm fat. **Diabetic Exchanges:** 2 starch, 1 vegetable, 1/2 fat. ***Editor's Note:** When cutting or seeding hot peppers, use rubber or plastic gloves to protect your hands. Avoid touching your face.

Berry Pineapple Parfaits

3 cups whole fresh strawberries
3 to 4 tablespoons sugar
12 scoops vanilla ice cream
1 can (8 ounces) crushed pineapple
Whipped topping

Reserve six strawberries for garnish. Slice the remaining strawberries and toss with sugar; let stand for 10 minutes. Spoon half of the sliced berries into six parfait glasses. Top with half of the ice cream and half of the pineapple. Repeat layers. Top with whipped topping and reserved strawberries. **Yield:** 6 servings.

Easy Equivalents
If you need 2 cups of shredded cooked chicken for a recipe, start with 3/4 pound boneless skinless chicken breasts or approximately 1-1/2 pounds bone-in chicken breasts.

GENERAL INDEX

✓ Recipe includes Nutritional Analysis and Diabetic Exchanges

✓ Recipe includes Nutritional Analysis and Diabetic Exchanges

ALPHABETICAL INDEX